THE WOLF
OF THE MIDDLE EAST

THE WOLF
OF THE MIDDLE EAST

HAKEEM AL-ZAYN

Command and Conquer LLC
Marlborough, MA

To the best of the author's knowledge, this work depicts actual events. While all persons within are actual individuals, some names and identifying characteristics have been changed to respect their privacy.

The Wolf of the Middle East copyright © 2022 by Hakeem Al-Zayn

Command and Conquer LLC
28 Church Street, Suite #14
Winchester, Massachusetts 01890

Publisher's Cataloging-In-Publication Data
    Names: Al-Zayn, Hakeem, author.
    Title: The wolf of the Middle East / Hakeem Al-Zayn.
    Description: Marlborough, MA : Command and Conquer LLC, [2022]
    Identifiers: ISBN: 979-8-9874390-0-5 (hardcover) | 979-8-9874390-1-2 (softcover) |

979-8-9874390-2-9 (ebook)

Subjects: LCSH: Robbery—Lebanon—History—20th century. | Criminals—Lebanon—Biography. | LCGFT: Biographies. | True crime stories. | BISAC: TRUE CRIME / Heists & Robberies. | BIOGRAPHY & AUTOBIOGRAPHY / Cultural, Ethnic & Regional / Arab & Middle Eastern. | BIOGRAPHY & AUTOBIOGRAPHY / Criminals & Outlaws.

Classification: LCC: HV6665.L4 A49 2022 | DDC: 364.1552095692—dc23

Contents

Tell Me What You Think

Let other readers know what you thought of *The Wolf of the Middle East*. Please write an honest review for this book on your favorite online bookshop.

★ ★ ★ ★ ★

Author's Note

The stories you are about to read are, to the best of my knowledge, true. While they are not my own, I am the only family member who was entrusted with them. Over the course of a few months, the man you'll meet related his entire life to me. The people, places, and perspectives within his stories were unlike any I'd ever heard before.

PROLOGUE

It all began in a hotel room by the sea.

There, a middle-aged, successful, alluring man named Hakeem—"the wise," in Arabic—practiced his only addiction with no boundaries. He represented his name in all aspects of life. But when it came to his lust, his sageness disappeared.

It was a Thursday night, 11:25 p.m., when his 12th floor hotel room doorbell rang.

"I was sent to you by Alex," said a fit, young, and beautiful, twenty-four-year-old woman.

Hakeem gazed at her soft figure, hugged tightly by a green velvet dress. Black strappy heels completed her ensemble.

"Is this your first time?" he asked

The girl did not respond—at first. She approached with a gentle touch on his shoulder. As she drew close, so close he could smell her light perfume, she stared straight into his eyes and said, "You'll find out," with a tiny grin.

The girl got down on her knees, unbelted his Louis Vuitton leather belt, unzipped his fly, and took it in with enthusiasm.

For Hakeem, time stopped. He couldn't move. He felt tied down by pleasure as he grew bigger and harder in her warm, soft mouth. She had it all done well with her long, silky tongue. He moved back. She stood and undressed him slowly. She helped herself to the bed, prompting him to show her what he had. Hakeem dove into every man's favorite destination. Surrounded by her, he couldn't last. One stroke . . . two strokes . . . three strokes . . . and that was it.

Hakeem closed his eyes, pulled out, and leaned in for a thank-you kiss. That's when he noticed how far down he'd ejaculated. A little bit made it inside. *One sperm.* By the time Hakeem woke from his bliss, it was too late. Little did he know what his uncontrolled desire seeded:

Not merely an unwanted child. But a child who would change......

CHAPTER 1

MISERY

One Year Later

The night was bitter and cold, Rain pattered through the empty streets, echoing to seemingly no one.

A slender, shadowed figure slid up the cobble street towards the orphanage's front gate. Looking around, it stepped through the opening and quickly strode to the front of the old building's crumbling facade.

The orphanage was a shamble of a building, surrounded by a roughly built stone wall. The cinder block walls had been painted over many times, but over the years, the colors had chipped and faded until it looked like a half-finished puzzle. The metal roof had deteriorated and rusted, leaving brown streaks of oxidation down the walls. At some point in history, the orphanage building had been used to house soldiers. Now it was only full of despair.

The shadow knocked on the door, and after a minute, there was a voice from inside.

"Who's there?"

"Open up . . . please . . ." pleaded the figure.

Slowly, the orphanage door cracked open, and the gatekeeper poked his head out. Above the door, a dim bulb cast just enough light to make out a young woman, fully covered with a niqab, holding a baby in her arms. Raindrops mixed with tears ran down her face.

He looked at the baby in her arms and knew why she was there.

"Are you sure you want to do this?" the gatekeeper asked.

The girl just nodded. He could see her eyes were red from crying, but nothing else showed behind the veil.

"I see. Does it have a name?"

"No." She shook her head.

The gatekeeper held out his arms. Gently, he took the baby from her. Within seconds, she vanished into the night. And she never looked back.

"So you have no name, eh, little one?" the gatekeeper cooed. Carefully unwrapping the blanket, he checked the baby for defects or injuries. Upon seeing it was a boy, he shook his head. "So you're a nobody? I guess I will call you something . . . special . . ."

He thought for a minute.

"Kamal."

Arabic for perfection.

The gatekeeper turned and closed the door behind him.

• • • •

"Leave Amir alone!" Kamal shouted and balled up his hands into fists.

A circle of boys, all bigger than Kamal, paused their assault on a poor scrawny kid in their midst. He was bloodied and battered, his arms purple from trying to defend himself.

"Shut up, Kamal, or you'll get it too!"

Kamal's mind raced. "He knows how to get sweet buns from the baker's wife!" Stepping closer, he pointed. "If you let him go, we can get you something good to eat."

As the bullies weighed Amir's fate, Kamal's stomach rumbled. He'd had nothing to eat in two days. To a growing thirteen-year-old, it felt like a week. Maybe two weeks. Time meant nothing. Constant, present hunger was the way of life.

The largest of the boys pulled up Amir by his shirt collar and threw him on the ground in front of Kamal. "You better find something," he roared. "Or we'll beat both of you!"

For a moment, Kamal waited for the bullies to be distracted by some other kid they could punish. He then quickly turned his attention to the bloody mess they had made of Amir.

"Amir, how bad are you hurt?"

Groaning, Amir managed to sit up. "I think I'm OK," he replied. "It looks worse than it is."

Kamal could feel his face burning with anger, but he knew there was nothing he could do for now. He helped Amir to his feet, and wrapping his arm around him, helped him hobble back to the orphanage's halls.

Once inside, Amir sat on his bare, filthy mattress—much like all the others in the room. Each sleeping quarter was packed full of mats and piles of scraps where children slept. Kamal quickly found a piece of ragged cloth, dipped it in some murky water from a pitcher, and began to carefully wipe the blood from Amir's face.

"Thanks for that," Amir said between gasps of pain. "I wasn't sure they were going to stop this time."

"It's OK," Kamal said soothingly. "We have to look out for each other." He patted Amir on the shoulder. "All we have is each other." He looked calm on the outside, but his rage continued to smolder.

Amir nodded. "I just wish you hadn't told them about the sweet buns," he said. "Now they're going to want something sweet all the time."

"If we can't find food, we're as good as dead anyway," Kamal reminded him. "We'll be lucky if they have enough for everyone to eat tonight. And I don't know about you," he added, "but I'm getting tired of bean water."

Amir chuckled. "Wouldn't it be wonderful if we stumbled upon a feast?"

Kamal agreed. "Maybe someday we will. Maybe someday."

• • • •

The air was still. A hint of noise and laughter wafted through the air. Kamal, Amir, and another boy, Mohammed, were crouched behind a fence. They spoke in hushed tones.

"I think we should split up," Kamal suggested. "We've got better chances of finding something that way."

"OK," Amir said. "You swing by the restaurants; I'll go through the rich people's alleys. Mo, you go around the docks. Maybe we'll get lucky."

Kamal nodded, and after a quick look around, darted off into the neighboring community, leaving Amir to circle around the dumpsters behind the line of restaurants down the street. Mo took off towards the dock warehouses.

About four blocks away, Kamal came across a row of opulent houses, some of which were close to the size of the orphanage. He knew these alleys well, and sometimes, if they were fortunate, there were discarded party leftovers that would feed them for days.

Working quickly and quietly, Kamal dug through pile after pile of garbage—some of it rather disgusting. Every now and then he'd come across a few bits of meat that hadn't gone bad, but most of it was too far gone to eat.

With a cry, he finally spotted his prize. Next to the dumpster, on the ground, was a half-opened can of tuna.

Stomach gurgling, Kamal slid down beside the dumpster and smelled the tuna. Still fresh, no flies. He peeled the lid back over the tuna and stuffed the can into his pocket. After making sure no one was around, he dashed through the alley and back on to the road, making his way towards the orphanage again.

Kamal kept his eyes peeled, but he didn't spot anything more until he had made it back to where Amir and Mo were anxiously waiting.

"Did you find anything?" Amir pleaded, his eyes sunken and longing. Mo's stomach rumbled.

Kamal nodded. "Did you?"

"I found half a meat and rice pita!" Amir held up a few squished, but intact, flatbread chunks.

"I got a couple of small fish," Mo said. "We can cook them later."

"I got something good too!" Kamal said, his eyes sparkling. "Look!" He pulled out the tuna

The look of amazement on Amir's face was worth putting up with the gnawing hunger. "Here, go ahead and eat it," Kamal insisted. "If we bring it back, they'll just steal it from us."

"Do you want some?" Amir asked, glancing at Mo. "You're hungry too."

"I've got my own fish," Mo said with a grin.

"You need to heal," Kamal insisted, shoving the tuna can into Amir's hands. "I can look for more tonight, dont worry about me!"

Amir nodded. Without hesitation, he ripped back the lid, barely bothering chewing before gulping it down.

Amir sighed deeply, enjoying the rare feeling of food in his belly. "Thank you, Kamal," he said with a smile. "I owe you one."

• • • •

Kamal woke to the sound of screams.

It took a few seconds for him to get his bearings, but when he opened his eyes, he was lying on his grimy mattress, back in the orphanage.

He turned his head to where Amir slept next to him, and his jaw dropped in horror.

Amir was kneeling on the floor, doubled over, violently retching. Saliva foamed around his mouth. His eyes were rolled back in his head.

Immediately, Kamal was by his side, holding him by the shoulders, trying to keep Amir from falling over. He realized the screaming had come from one of the other boys in their room—there were half a dozen standing there, pointing, whispering in hushed tones, but none dared intervene.

"Amir! AMIR!" Kamal sounded, to no avail. The vomiting continued, violently, as Amir's entire body wracked with convulsions. After what seemed like an eternity, Amir passed out. His hands still shook. Both of their shirts were covered in vomit.

The orphanage director, a somber middle-aged woman, appeared in the doorway from the commotion. She was dressed plainly and had her hair pulled up in a bun. Her face wasn't necessarily unattractive, but everything about her screamed mediocrity. Average height, average build, and hawkish eyes that saw everything. Her defining feature was a scar that ran the length of her left cheek.

She took a few steps towards them to get a glimpse of Amir's condition, remaining more than an arm's reach away. Kamal carefully laid Amir down on his mat and looked up. The director's expression turned cold.

"What happened?" she inquired. "What's wrong? Kamal?"

Still reeling from the shock, Kamal shook his head. "I don't know!" he cried, his voice cracking. "We found some tuna earlier, and . . ."

"Tuna?" the director repeated. "Where did you find it?"

Kamal looked down at Amir, who had stopped shaking, but was still breathing. Each jagged breath was punctuated with a rasp. His entire body had broken out in sweats.

"We were looking for food that people had thrown away and I found a can just laying there on the ground!" He shrugged. "It was like someone had left it for us."

"*Tsk-tsk*." The director slowly shook her head. "You stupid little boy. Kamal, do you know why they do that?"

Kamal just stared back at her.

"They leave open cans of tuna out for the wild feral cats to find," she said. "They've been poisoned."

"Poison?" Kamal silently mouthed. His mind reeled. Someone had tried to poison us? No—she had said feral cats.

"Why would they do that?" Kamal begged to know.

"Mostly, to keep the population in check." She frowned. "Those cats are vicious."

Somehow, Kamal knew she wasn't just talking about cats. "Shouldn't we bring him to the doctor?" he pleaded. "He's really sick!"

"Amir is a strong boy," she said, shaking her head. "He'll probably feel better in the morning."

"Why not?!" Kamal yelled. "He needs a doctor!"

"There's nothing we can do for him," she replied calmly. "Let him rest. That's his best hope."

Kamal wanted to fight, to kick, to scream; but it would do no good. So he wiped his eyes, did his best to wipe off his shirt, and walked to the kitchen. He grabbed a large mug, dipped it in the rain cistern just outside, and brought it back to their room. The other children, suspecting the worst, kept their distance.

For the next few hours, Kamal tended to his best friend. He wiped his forehead, dabbed his face with water to try to revive him, and attempted to make him comfortable.

Briefly, Amir would come to his senses and drink a sip of water. But as the night wore on, his skin grew pale and yellowed, and his speech became less intelligible. Even in his sleep, Amir would occasionally whimper like a wounded animal.

Kamal's gut twisted into knots watching Amir suffer. He fought to stay awake, but as the hours dragged on, his exhaustion finally drew him into dark and restless sleep.

• • • •

With a start, Kamal jolted awake. It was still mostly dark, but the faintest hint of daybreak had begun to creep into the grimy window. There were no screams, no noises. In fact, it was unnaturally silent.

Sitting up, Kamal realized he was cold and wet—mostly from Amir's vomit. The smell was absolutely putrid. He did his best to not breathe through his nose.

Kamal stood and went to the window. As he drew back the faded curtain, orange sunrise came through the grimy panes, illuminating the room.

He quickly returned to Amir's side. But as soon as he saw him, he knew.

All the color had drained from Amir's body. His entire torso was crusted with dried vomit and food, and flies had begun to respond to the smell. But there was no movement—no life left in Amir's body. His jagged breathing had stopped. There were no more whimpers or moans, no more laughter or smiles.

Amir was dead.

Kamal's face burned hot as anger, his eyes started flowing with tears, grief, and hatred boiled up inside him. It crested, overflowed, and poured out through a single, haunting wail that echoed throughout the orphanage complex.

At that exact moment, Kamal felt total pain. His heart ached. His body hurt. Then that pain descended into hatred. For everyone. For the director, the orphanage, the country he lived in, the mother who abandoned him, for the rich people who poisoned his one and only friend. He hated everyone. Life itself was one big cruel joke—at Kamal's expense.

• • • •

It had been four years since Amir had died, and not a single day had gone by without Kamal thinking about him. But today was different.

A new face had appeared that morning—a young girl, possibly fourteen or fifteen years old, had showed up at the orphanage. She was accompanied by an older couple who bickered back and forth as they conversed with the director.

Any time a new kid showed up, there was talk. But this time, the chatter among the children was spreading fast. Kamal decided he would see for himself.

A lot of orphans were dropped there as infants or were discovered on the streets if they survived long enough. It was rare to see someone come in with people.

Kamal's curiosity got the better of him, and he approached the edge of the yard where the couple was standing, talking with the director. The girl just stood there behind them, silent.

Once he was close enough Kamal began to make out some of the conversation.

". . . she cannot remain with us," the older lady was saying. "Can you take her—yes or no?"

The director sighed. "We have very little space for the number of children we have, but we can do our best to take care . . ."

Kamal strained, but could hear no more. He stepped around the corner and glimpsed a peek at them again and saw that the girl was actually very pretty. Something about her made his heart move.

"Why would a pretty girl like her be left here?" Kamal thought to himself. But the answer would have to wait.

• • • •

"Leave her alone!" Kamal shouted. For a moment, he felt some sort of déjà vu.

The three girls that had cornered the newcomer turned and glared at Kamal. He was no longer the runt of the orphanage, though he still wasn't very liked by bullies.

"Why do you care, Kamal?" one of them taunted.

Kamal took two steps forward and raised his fist, grasping a knife tightly in it. "I said leave her alone." His face did not waver or show any hesitation.

"Fine," the girl spat, and the three of them slunk away, leaving the new girl standing alone in the corner of the courtyard.

Kamal looked at her. Her sweatpants and t-shirt were clean. She didn't look malnourished or sickly. In fact, she was very well-kept.

"Th—thank you," she squeaked, her voice still shaky from the confrontation.

"Are you OK?" Kamal asked. "What did they do?"

"They were teasing me and pulling my hair," she said, barely keeping from crying.

"You've only been here a few days, and they're already at it." He frowned. "Don't worry. If they bother you, just let me know."

"Thank you!" she gasped. "I'm very scared here. Some of the boys tried to push me around . . . tried to . . . touch me . . ."

Kamal scowled. "What do you mean?"

"They were putting their hands all over me," she whispered. "Trying to push me to the ground. I was too afraid to tell anyone, but they were saying really nasty things to me. I was afraid they were going to do things to me."

"They would definitely hurt you," Kamal said. "You need to try not to let them corner you. It's dangerous."

"I—I didn't know," she said as tears rolled down her cheeks. "It's so different here."

"Can I ask you something?" Kamal said quietly.

She just nodded.

"How did you end up here? What happened to you?"

"My parents were married without their parent's approval," she said. "I loved them very much. But they both died in a car crash. Just days ago." She closed her eyes for a second, then added, "Nobody in the family wanted to take me."

Something inside Kamal shifted. "I wish I could make everything better." He just stared for a moment. "What's your name?"

"Nicolette."

· · · ·

Months later, the orphanage was bustling with excitement. An extraordinarily rich donor to the orphanage had appeared, and everyone was talking about him. There were whispers of some kid being lucky enough to be adopted by him and speculations over what kind of businesses he ran. Someone said he owned all the factories in town. Another said he was a high-ranking government official.

He had heard about the "rich old man," but he hadn't seen him yet. Kamal had been busy rummaging through shops and such, looking for something special. Nicolette's sixteenth birthday was coming up, and he wanted to find something special for her. Maybe something as simple as a ribbon for her hair, or if he was lucky, some trinkets, or a little decorated box—anything to make her feel welcomed.

"Did you hear?" Nicolette bubbled. "They're going to throw me a birthday party!"

Kamal smiled. "I didn't think they had enough money to do a party."

"Well, the director said that the old man would pay for it." Nicolette grinned. "Can you believe it?"

Kamal's mind raced with bad thoughts, but he didn't want to ruin something that brought her joy. "That's . . . that's amazing." he finally managed.

"I'm so happy for you"

Kamal just nodded.

· · · ·

When the day of the party arrived, there was a general buzz of excitement among the children. If there was a party, that meant they would get something good to eat.

The main dinner hall was decorated with a few streamers, and a simple tablecloth was laid across the center table. As children started filing in, Kamal made his way through the group and picked a chair relatively close to the middle. Somewhere in the background, he could hear music playing from an old radio.

The director and Nicolette entered, followed by a man, roughly in his late forties, with thinning hair and a wide mustache. Kamal noticed the man's eyes were shifting constantly. He could tell a lot about a person from their eyes.

"Today," said the director loudly, "thanks to a generous friend, we're going to do something special!"

The gathered children murmured excitedly. One of the kitchen workers brought out a rather large cake, to much *oohing* and *aahing*. Kamal's stomach rumbled in response.

"Today is our sweet Nicolette's sixteenth birthday!" the director exclaimed. "And not only that," she added, pointing to the man, "but Mr. Farouk has decided to adopt her! Let's celebrate together."

Watching Nicolette beaming with happiness made Kamal's heart jump. He didn't know why he felt so protective over her—certainly she was pretty, but there was more to it than that.

The director led them in singing a birthday song, and everyone clapped while the kitchen help began cutting the cake into slices for the children. Nicolette sat at the table with the director and the businessman, Mr. Farouk. Kamal kept his eyes on him, and every now and then he would lean in to say something in Nicolette's ear. Something about the way he put his hand on her shoulder made him uneasy.

The cake lasted until the children were satisfied, and they slowly dispersed as the excitement wound down, and they began cleaning the dining hall. The director stood and motioned for Nicolette and Mr. Farouk to follow her into her office, which was the adjoining room. Some paperwork had to be finished, she said.

Kamal was one of the last to leave, and as they filed out the door, he turned and quickly slipped around the corner, doubling back to the other side of the hall. He watched closely as the three went into the director's office. The door shut behind them. Faintly, Kamal could make out their speech but couldn't understand the conversation. After a minute, the director opened the door and left, headed to the front of the building.

Sensing his opportunity, Kamal waited until the last kitchen staff had left, and crept over to the door. Silently, he turned and placed his ear on the door.

"Aren't you happy?" he could hear the man saying.

"Yes . . ." Nicolette trailed off.

Kamal strained to hear.

"Come closer. You look so tense."

Kamal then heard some noise, like something being moved, but he couldn't tell what. Then a muffled voice, increasing in intensity. Some more shuffling, something falling . . .

Suddenly, a half-muffled scream came through, quite clearly. Kamal's blood ran cold.

He grabbed the doorknob and twisted, but it didn't budge—it had been locked.

The screaming suddenly stopped. There was more banging and what sounded like a struggle.

Panic rising, Kamal took three steps back, and with every ounce of strength in him, threw himself at the door, aiming his shoulder right above the doorknob.

There was a loud bang. The door jamb gave way. Kamal tumbled into the room, taking a second to gain his bearings.

There in front of him was Mr. Farouk. He was half kneeling, half standing on the sofa, his pants around his knees, with Nicolette beneath him. Farouk had pinned her arms above her head with one hand, and was covering her mouth with the other. He had managed to force himself between her legs, and was in the middle of violently raping her.

The man's eyes were feral, like an animal that had caught a prize kill. Nicolette's face was streaked with tears. Kamal could see blood on the sofa, blood all over their legs, and blood running down Farouk's arms from where Nicolette had scratched him. With every thrust she let out a muffled shriek of pain, interspersed with wails of fear and misery. Her cries grew weaker as she was slowly starved of oxygen. Seconds later, Farouk let out a loud groan, pushing himself into her with all his strength, nearly breaking her wrists from the effort.

"NO!" Kamal shouted and instinctively pulled his knife from his pocket. With lightning-fast reflexes, he dashed forward and plunged the knife into the man's lower back as hard as he could.

The man yelped in pain and swatted Kamal aside with a strong blow, but the knife had done its job. Blood flowed everywhere as the man jumped up, pulled the knife from below his ribs, and threw it aside. He stumbled, managed to mostly pull his pants back up, and bolted for the door.

Kamal managed to stand up and catch his breath, but the man was gone before he could do anything.

Realizing Nicolette was still there, he looked away as she pulled her dress down. Tears welled in her eyes.

"Are you OK?"

Nicolette turned white.

Just then, the director stormed through the broken door, hands on her hips, and fire in her eyes. "What happened?" she demanded.

Nicolette couldn't speak. She slumped over on the couch. Eyes glazed over. Her gaze took her away. Far away. She looked almost . . . dead. Dead as Amir the morning Kamal found his body.

My fault, this . . . it's my fault . . . again . . .

"I—I heard her scream," Kamal managed. "So I broke the door open and caught him."

"Why did you scare off the most important man you've ever met?" the director shouted. "Why is there blood all over my couch?" She glared at Kamal. "You filthy rat!" And she smacked him across the face.

CHAPTER 2

ESCAPE

"He will pay for what he did," Kamal seethed. "So will the director. They'll both pay with everything they have."

The poor girl's eyes, still red and dripping grief, fueled his fury even more.

So what happens now?!

Kamal thought until his head ached. His mind raced through scenarios, each more morbid than the last. There *had* to be some way to make things right. But even if not, he couldn't allow Nicolette to be hurt again, no matter what. Not ever.

Then, just as quickly as his anger had risen, Kamal's head cleared.

"I can't erase it—but I can prevent it from happening again." His cold stare never wavered. "Not to you."

Nicolette said nothing for a long moment. "How?" She finally managed.

"Don't worry about that."

• • • •

Kamal got the old bicycle's wheels turning. Barely. The brakes didn't work, the seat was falling off, and the tires wobbled. But it would work.

As he crouched behind a row of bushes, Kamal could make out the director exiting the orphanage gate, towards her car. It wasn't a fancy car, an old Mercedes, but that was to be expected of someone who ran a government orphanage.

As daylight faded, the car pulled away and ambled down the road. Kamal quickly mounted the bike and followed, keeping to the edge of the road where he wasn't that visible to her.

Several turns later he had trailed the car to the edge of the river, where a large sidewalk wound along. He pedaled furiously to keep up. Though she wasn't going that fast, he was afraid the bike would fall apart under him. It held, however, and after thirty minutes and several kilometers, they reached a large intersection at the bottom of a hill. To the left was a sharp drop into the valley. The car slowed and turned right, away from the river, up a steep, winding street into a residential neighborhood.

Winded, Kamal stashed the bike and followed on foot, keeping an eye on the car's tail lights. He climbed the hill as fast as his tired legs would allow, cutting across the curves to keep up. When the car finally stopped in front of a rather nice two-story home, he memorized the address.

After the director left the car and entered her home, Kamal caught his breath and retreated back down the street. At the bottom of the hill, he recovered his bike, and then made his way back to the orphanage. By the time he arrived, it was pitch black outside, and no one noticed him casually walking through.

For the next few days, Kamal rose early while most of the children were still asleep. The director would usually arrive at the orphanage within an hour after daybreak. She'd park in the same place, throw her bag over her shoulder, and march inside. He'd watch her pull her keys out of the bag, unlock the door to her office, and close it behind her.

Taking the money from the vault would mean the orphanage would be left without any funds. Kamal knew she kept it in a safe inside her office, but he didn't have a clue how to get into it. *Yet.* He knew the keys to the safe were in her bag, but it never left her side. There was no way he could get away with assaulting her to get it, either.

Every day, the director went about her duties, and Kamal watched and followed. Around noon, she would shoulder her satchel and drive into town to get lunch from a local deli. Sometimes she would run a few errands, sometimes not. Kamal knew every route she took, every place she stopped.

He noticed that if the weather was nice, she would drive around with her windows down. And that next morning the weather was beautiful, so Kamal decided to make his move.

A couple hours after breakfast, Kamal snuck outside and hopped over the courtyard wall to retrieve the old bicycle he'd stashed. He mounted it and headed for the center of town where he knew the director would soon be going.

Twenty minutes later, Kamal slowed as he approached the familiar busy intersection. He moved to the sidewalk and stopped when he had a clear view of the southern approaching traffic. There was a ninety-nine percent chance the director would drive right by him. He grabbed a bandana from his pocket and secured it around his neck.

After just a couple of minutes, he spotted her faded old Mercedes roughly three blocks away. It was time. Moving into the crosswalk, Kamal gave his pedals three hard rotations, and slammed straight into the side of a car waiting its turn at the intersection. Kamal flung himself off his bike and sprawled himself out on all fours in front of the stopped car. The driver of an approaching red sedan slammed on his brakes just in front of Kamal, then a silver convertible rear ended the sedan.

For a moment, everyone froze at the site of the accident. Suddenly, the drivers were all sticking their heads out of their windows, frantically yelling at each other over the fender bender. Almost unnoticed, Kamal rolled away and slid back onto the bike. All the confusion, shouting, and cars honking was the perfect diversion. He slipped through the throngs of agitated drivers and pedestrians until he was ten meters from the director's car.

Kamal hopped off the bike and knelt down in the street as if tying his shoe. He raised the bandana over his face. He stayed down until the director's car slowed to a stop right beside him.

Taking a deep breath, Kamal raised into a half-crouch and reached into the open passenger window. The director's bag was exactly where he thought it would be. He slid his hand through the strap, swung it out the window, then swung his leg back over the bike. He was flying away from the street before anyone knew what had happened.

Over the rest of the commotion, he heard the director's voice screeching from far behind him.

"COME BACK HERE!"

But her protests were lost in the clamor of the intersection.

He kept pedaling until his legs were begging him to stop. He was at least three kilometers from the accident now—far enough away that he could relax a little. Nobody had followed him, as far as he could tell. The director had probably been unable to get through the huge crowd of angry people, and she wouldn't have left her car in the middle of the street.

Kamal slowed as he reached the mouth of an alley. Turning sharply, he caught a pothole just around the corner. He didn't see it. He couldn't have. Kamal hurled forwards off his bike as the front wheel crunched into itself.

"What's this?" someone called out before Kamal could check himself for cuts.

It was a police officer.

What were the chances?

The bandana and woman's purse gave Kamal away. Before Kamal's adult life even started, it was about to be over. Nicolette would be alone. Forever.

But he promised.

"Thief! Street rat!" The cop lunged towards Kamal, still on his back.

One sudden kick at the officer's groin sent him tumbling down. He let out a scream, but Kamal was gone. He had time to grab only the bag. The bike was no more. So was any chance of arrest by the time Kamal's legs finally gave out.

• • • •

On the other side of town, Kamal collapsed into a pile of trash for a breather. Finally, it was safe to check the director's bag. Inside were her wallet, some papers, a colorful scarf, and . . . a set of keys.

Kamal pocketed the keys and emptied the wallet, taking what little cash was there. He picked out the director's driver's license, and double-checked the address.

Kamal followed the streets until he reached the director's street at the top of the hill. He spotted her house and saw her car parked in her driveway. That meant she hadn't gone back to the orphanage. She'd gone straight home, right where Kamal wanted her to be.

Kamal looked around for anyone who could have seen him, but the street was empty and quiet. He quickly squatted down and slid underneath the director's car, and pulled a pair of small wire cutting pliers from his pocket.

For the last few weeks, Kamal had been spending time hanging out at the local mechanic's shop, shadowing one of the younger mechanics that used to live at the orphanage. He had learned quite a bit from him about how cars worked in general, and they had even let him turn a few wrenches when no one was looking. He had asked questions about what happened when things failed. Specifically, when a car's brakes failed.

Looking around below, he could barely see, but managed to identify the car's brake lines running to each wheel. Kamal positioned himself to where he could reach a line with both hands. He put the pliers on the rubber part of the line that went from the frame to the wheel, and cut a slice partway through it. He could see dark red fluid oozing from the incision. The brakes would still work, for a while, until the fluid ran out. Squirming further under the car, he found the hose on the opposite wheel, and nicked it as well.

His work done, Kamal slid himself out from under the vehicle and brushed himself off. It was late, and it was going to take him a while to make it back to the orphanage, but Kamal didn't mind.

By the time Kamal got back to the orphanage, it was dark. He stashed his bandana and hopped back over the wall. There was no sign of anyone outside.

He knocked on the door of Nicolette's shared room. "Come in," came a quiet voice from inside.

Slowly, he opened the door. The lights were off and the room was dark. "Nicolette, it's me."

"Kamal. I thought you left," she whispered.

"I would never leave you. Are you all right?"

She quietly approached the door where Kamal could see her, and nodded. Kamal could tell she hadn't left the room in a while—her hair was everywhere, her clothes were rumpled, and her eyes looked sunken and cold. She looked much different from the innocent little girl he used to know.

"Get some sleep," he insisted. "I'll see you again in the morning."

That night, Kamal waited patiently. After everything was closed up and all the children were in their rooms, he waited another hour until he was sure everyone had drifted off to sleep. Then he silently slipped out of his room.

The halls were pitch dark, but Kamal knew them like the back of his hand. He crossed the courtyard to the office building, barely able to see his own feet in the moonlight.

Inside the office building, he passed a few storage rooms and a small waiting room. As Kamal snuck down the hallway, every nerve was on edge. Getting caught would mean severe punishment.

He rounded the corner and froze. Footsteps echoed through the doorway ahead of him. Kamal glanced around for someplace to hide, but the only thing he could do was duck inside an open closet.

The steps drew closer, but Kamal quickly realized the steps were too close together to be the night watchman. His suspicion was confirmed as one of the orphanage boys walked past, most likely to go use the bathroom. Kamal waited patiently until the coast was clear, but his heart was still racing. He had been lucky up to this point, but there was always the possibility that his luck would run out.

Eventually he reached the director's office. He slowly pulled the keys from his pocket, making sure not to let them jingle. He found one that looked like a door key, and sure enough, it slid into the doorknob effortlessly. He entered and closed the door behind him.

Kamal made straight for the cabinet in the corner. It was a cheap metal one, about the size of a small filing cabinet. It didn't have a fancy combination lock like an actual safe. It was really just a beefy filing drawer, with a heavy padlock on it. He put another key into the lock, and it popped open on the first try.

Inside, he found a cardboard box of cash and stacks of manila folders. He stuffed the cash in his pockets and left everything else.

Kamal carefully closed everything back exactly the way he had found it. He paused for a second, listening, but everything was still completely silent except for his heart beating in his chest.

He locked the office door on his way out, careful not to touch anything that would indicate someone had been there. He left the building, made his way back across the courtyard, and finally back to the room where the other boys were still sound asleep.

Kamal hastily shoved the cash into his backpack, making sure to bury it beneath the other items he'd stashed in there—his jacket, some twine, an old knife blade he'd found, and a few other things. There was a lot of cash, but he hadn't taken the time to count it all. Rough estimate, probably several months' worth of apartment rent. More than enough to get him started.

Finally, he laid down on the filthy mattress and closed his eyes. Memories of Amir passed through his mind, and as he remembered, any concerns he might have had for the orphanage, or the director, faded quickly. He decided not to concern himself with what happened—as long as he could leave with Nicolette.

• • • •

When daylight broke, Kamal woke up with a start. He was exhausted, having only slept a few hours. Boys were milling around, murmuring. There were curious looks, whispers, and a lot of energy. Fleetingly, Kamal wondered if they had discovered the missing money, but his fears were relieved when he overheard some of the boys.

"She's not here?"

"No. The gatekeeper says she never showed up this morning."

"You sure?"

"Of course! Go look for yourself!"

Kamal stood, shouldered his backpack, and left the room without a word. He walked through the hallway until he reached the main dining hall, where there were groups of children sitting at the tables. They looked like they had assembled for breakfast—meager as it was—but instead of being served, the kitchen staff was nowhere to be seen.

He scanned the room for Nicolette, and not seeing her, left and crossed the breezeway to the girl's wing. He passed a few more kids huddled together, but no one made eye contact. Kamal suspected Nicolette

THE WOLF OF THE MIDDLE EAST

was still in her room, so he knocked on the door as usual, and this time, it swung open.

Nicolette was standing there alone, still looking very tired and hungry, but she was at least dressed.

"Kamal!" She blinked and rubbed her eyes. "You're here early."

"We missed breakfast. Let's go get something to eat." Kamal reached out, firmly took hold of her hand, and pulled her towards the door.

Nicolette resisted briefly, took a quick look behind her, and then stepped out into the hall.

"Should I grab my bag?"

"No," Kamal said. "Just come with me."

"OK."

Kamal led her out to the courtyard, where the children were gathered around the spot where the director's car was usually parked. While they looked for clues, Kamal just headed for the front gate with Nicolette in tow.

They stopped at the gate. The gatekeeper, the same one who had been there since before Kamal was dropped off, who had named him, was standing there. He was busy talking to another man, maybe a reporter or a detective. They exchanged a few sentences, and the man nodded and left.

Kamal approached the gatekeeper.

"What happened?" Kamal asked.

"Nothing." The old man looked Kamal up and down and raised an eyebrow. "Are you going somewhere?"

"We're going to find breakfast," Kamal replied.

"Very well. Be safe."

Kamal just nodded, and with a tug, led Nicolette through the gate into the street. They walked for a few blocks, eventually coming upon a small cart selling food, next to a storefront. Through the store's window, Kamal could see several televisions, some of which were on. His stomach rumbled at the smell coming from the cart.

"I'd like two fatayer, please," he said to the vendor, who nodded, and began pulling things out of the cart's container.

"I'm not hungry," Nicolette said.

"You have to try to eat. Here, try something."

Kamal handed her a large meat pie wrapped in paper. He then pulled out some bills from his pocket, paid the vendor, and took a fatayer as well.

They took a few steps to where the store's window overhang shaded them from the morning sun, and Kamal took a huge bite, savoring the taste of freshly cooked crust. The scent filled his nostrils as the warm feta cheese slid down his throat, making his head spin with flavor.

"This is so good. Why don't you try a bite?"

Nicolette just looked at the wrap, her eyes vacant.

"Look, Nicolette . . ." Kamal moved to where he was standing directly in front of her, and put his hand on her shoulder. "You have to wake up. There's nothing there for us anymore. We're going to make a new life."

"What are we going to do?"

"I have enough money to last us for a while. We can buy real food. We can have a place for ourselves, without sharing rooms."

For once, Nicolette's eyes brightened, and she looked into Kamal's eyes with peace. Finally, she could rest.

"I just need you to eat something so you'll have the energy to go look for an apartment." Kamal pointed to her fatayer. "Are you going to try it?"

Nicolette looked at it, then handed it back to him. "Not yet. Not right now."

"If you say so." He carefully placed the fatayer in his backpack. As he looked up and smiled, he could see one of the store's television sets over Nicolette's shoulder.

He recognized the director's car on the screen. The headline underneath it read:

STATE WORKER KILLED IN BRAKE FAILURE ACCIDENT
ON WAY TO WORK

A feeling of intense calm washed over Kamal. "This is how it is now," he thought to himself. "Killing people that deserve to die." They had taken advantage of innocent children, abused them, treated them like the garbage and filth they forced them to live in. Nobody deserved to be treated that way by anyone.

Kamal turned and looked at Nicolette's face. He wouldn't just kill for her- he would burn the whole world down for her if that was what she wanted.

Nicolette turned, and gasped. "Is that . . . " The TV flashed a picture of the orphanage director on the screen, while a news anchor gave details of the accident.

" . . . *careened down a steep hill, breaking through barriers and landing upside-down in the river. and no one else was in the car at the time . . . "*

Nicolette turned back to face Kamal, and several conflicting emotions flashed across her face.

"What did you do?"

Kamal just shrugged, and took a bite of fatayer.

"Wait—did you . . . "

"I don't know what you're talking about," Kamal said.

Nicolette's face was now a mix of shock and confusion.

"Sometimes," Kamal said calmly, still chewing, "people who are involved in bad things meet untimely deaths." He stared off. "Maybe it was all fate."

"Fate?"

"My type of fate."

"And you did all this . . . for me?"

"For us," he said, swallowing another bite. "Are you hungry yet? What do you say?"

Nicolette smiled weakly and nodded.

"I think I'm ready."

"Good." He handed her the wrapped fatayer, and pointed away from the store, in the direction of the center of town.

"Let's go. I hear there's some affordable places over that way."

• • • •

Days later, the entire orphanage had been gathered for the director's burial. All the children, about a hundred, were lined up in rows. Kamal and Nicolette stood in the back where they could see everyone but no one could see them. The children weren't allowed to look in the casket, Kamal knew, because the accident had been so bad.

"Dear children, today we celebrate a life of service and dedication . . ."

Kamal looked around. Most of the children were either bored, or aggravated that they had to stand still. But to Kamal, this was the ultimate trophy: he had gotten revenge for the director allowing Amir's death, Nicolette's rape, and who knew how many other crimes.

"Finally," Kamal whispered to Nicolette, "she won't be responsible for any more deaths."

Nicolette just nodded, her eyes filled with tears.

Deep inside, Kamal was glad, but he wouldn't be satisfied until he had taken his revenge on everyone that had done him wrong.

CHAPTER 3

ORIGINS

"It's just a studio. But it'll do."

Kamal had managed to find something in town, but there weren't many large places available to rent. The room was fairly big, but contained everything, including a sleeping area and a tiny kitchen. The walls were covered in ancient wallpaper, but at least had been recently scrubbed. The cheap vinyl flooring was worn in places, and the furniture all looked at least twenty years old.

Nicolette entered and walked up to the single window overlooking an alley.

"I like it," she said. "It even has furniture."

Kamal nodded. "It's only one room though, so I'll sleep on the couch."

Nicolette looked around and frowned. "Won't you, um, isn't that . . ."

"Don't worry. I'll get some dividers so you can have your own space."

Nicolette blushed a little, but quickly turned and flopped down on the bed. "Finally! A real bed again!" Memories of her childhood home flooded her mind. At last, she had her own bed again.

"We can stay here for a while, but we're going to have to work on getting some more money eventually." Kamal knew the only way to make real money was to get involved with people who were accustomed to a rich lifestyle, but the only people he knew were beggars and thieves. He needed to find a way to blend in with people who had money.

He could see Nicolette's breathing slow as she finally relaxed. For the first time in two days, Nicolette drifted off to sleep.

Kamal looked down at Nicolette sprawled on the bed, her hair spread all around, and immediately looked away. He couldn't think of her that way. His feelings could not be allowed to dictate his life. Not any more.

• • • •

As Kamal was returning from the store, there was a commotion across the street. A couple was arguing loudly and making a scene. The man was wearing a very nice cotton suit, sunglasses, and a hat with a wide brim. The woman, who was noticeably younger than the man and dressed just as nicely, was waving her hands around and raising her voice. They were arguing in a language he didn't know, so he guessed they were tourists.

Kamal watched with interest as the woman, apparently upset with something the man had done, slung her handbag around her shoulder and stomped off, head held high. She stormed across the street and passed right by Kamal without giving him so much as a glance.

As the woman walked by, it struck him: *Who has money in a beach town? Tourists at resorts.* And with a major resort just a few miles down the coast, he started to form a plan.

Over the next few weeks, Kamal spent his afternoons along the beach, circulating through the boardwalks, and watching people. He would ride his bicycle down the coast to where a large walled resort was always crowded with tourists. He saw all kinds of foreign businessmen there: glamorous Qataris, Saudi princes, the elite of UAE. They were all relaxed and enjoying themselves. Kamal saw only easy targets.

Entrance to the resort wasn't restricted, so Kamal walked around the sprawling courtyards and pools, taking note of everything. He followed the people who looked like they had the most money—gold chains, nice watches, expensive suits, girlfriends with designer handbags. There was always a stream of workers milling about, each one with a nametag, a crisp pair of white shorts, and a starched white button-down shirt. Some were towel boys, some were waitresses, some were room service.

As he passed the main resort tower, he noticed the enormous outdoor pool was always busy and had lots of people coming and going. Next to the door was a sign with the usual list of rules, in Arabic and English. But at the very bottom of the sign, something specific caught Kamal's eye: *Non-Guests Must Pay For Pool Access.*

He quickly made his way to the service desk and inquired about the pool fee, which ended up being more reasonable than he'd thought. Kamal promptly pulled out his wallet and paid the fee for a month, thanked the clerk, and took the access card they gave him.

Kamal made his way back to the pool, and after flashing his pass at the person behind the kiosk, walked outside. It was a beautiful Olympic-sized pool, bordered with decorative tiles, and surrounded by deck chairs. The smell of chlorinated water immediately stung his nose. People milled about talking, as towel boys darted around them like ants. A few children splashed and squealed with delight in nearby smaller, shallow pools.

Kamal decided to make a lap around the cavernous room, making notes of where each exit was. It was a bit harder to tell who the very rich people were when everyone was in bathing suits, but every now and then, he would catch a glimpse of gold or a flash of diamonds. He also noticed that several of the businessmen would leave their belongings on the tables in between the deck chairs—sometimes even leaving them there while they went down to the beach. A quick glance revealed keys, wallets, watches, and more, completely unattended.

Everyone seemed focused on their jobs, and Kamal was able to move through the place relatively unnoticed.

When he had finished his round, he left the pool and walked back outside. Passing through the resort gate, Kamal saw the hour was getting late, and decided he would return the next day. He would have to make a stop at the department store first, though.

• • • •

The next morning, as soon as the shops opened, Kamal was waiting. He entered a clothing store and approached the counter.

"Hello. Where can I find white shirts and white shorts?"

The clerk pointed out a rack of clothing along the back wall. "All the white clothes are over there."

THE WOLF OF THE MIDDLE EAST

"Thank you." He sorted through them for a few minutes, and bought three crisp, white shorts, three white polo shirts, and white shoes. He had to ask where to find a name tag, but was quickly directed to an office supply shop next door, where he purchased a blank badge and some lettering to put on it.

When he was done, he brought the stash back to the apartment where Nicolette was just stirring. As he entered, she sat up and yawned.

"I got some uniforms, just like the ones they use at the resort." He held up his collection to show her.

"You? A working man?"

"Don't be silly," Kamal said with a smile. With that, he folded the uniforms and put two sets of them away. He then took the rest of it and changed in the bathroom.

When he emerged, Nicolette giggled. "You look like a pool boy!"

"Exactly." He glanced at himself in the mirror. It was just what he needed.

• • • •

Back at the resort, Kamal quickly got to work. He followed some of the staffers around, watching what they did, so he could mimic them. He also made sure to stay away from the main desk so he wouldn't be spotted by an inquisitive manager.

After a little while, he followed a couple of boys carrying towels into the pool area. They dropped off their piles, picked up a few empty glasses and plates from the tables, and left through the side entrance.

Kamal spotted a table on the other side of the pool that had several tables littered with glasses. There was a rather fat, old man lounging there, wearing large gold chains. He was chatting up some young girl in a swimsuit.

Kamal waited until he saw the two of them get up and head towards the stairs leading down to the beach. He knew if they went down there, they wouldn't be back for a while.

A few more seconds, and they had gone through the doors. Kamal smoothly walked around the pool until he got to their table. Among the towels, glasses, and plates piled there, he could see the man's keys and wallet. One of the keys was on a hotel room keychain, with a room number tag on it.

Kamal picked up the plates, a few glasses, and grabbed the hotel key. He slowly made his way around the pool until he saw one of the other pool boys pass through. Kamal quickly decided to follow him, but at a distance. Through the side entrance, a hallway branched off in two directions, split by a table. He quickly dumped the dishes on the table and stored through the hall, back around to the main courtyard.

The elevators were central to the building, so Kamal went around the back to where the stairwell was. Once he was climbing the stairs, he pulled the hotel key out and looked at it. The number "309" was embossed in gold. He kept climbing until he reached the third floor and exited the stairwell.

There was no one around that he could see, so Kamal followed the hall around until he reached Room 309. He knocked, just in case there was someone inside, but there was no answer.

He unlocked the door, stepped inside, and looked around. It was very lavish. Glancing around, he could see briefcases, suitcases, and some clothes left lying out. The closet was open. Above some hanging shirts on a shelf was a small safe.

It was a key safe that the hotel had provided so customers could lock up their belongings while they were away from the room. Kamal used the smaller key on the key ring, and with a click, the safe swung open.

He was greeted with several large stacks of bills and a diamond necklace.

Kamal distributed the cash and jewelry into all his pockets so it wouldn't be noticeable to the casual observer. Making a quick count, he was surprised to find there was easily twice as much cash as he had stolen from the orphanage. He carefully closed the safe and left the room, making sure to leave everything as he had found it.

Standing in the hallway, Kamal looked around, but the place was still empty. He spotted a "Room Service" hanger on another door nearby, grabbed it, and hung it on room 309's doorknob. Room service would then check the room during their daily rounds, placing them at the scene of the robbery. It was very likely that someone in the room service staff would take the blame and possibly even go to jail.

As the thought crossed his mind, he felt nothing but cold, dark indifference. He had ended up in an orphanage through no fault of his own, his life effectively ruined in society's eyes. No one had cared about whether he lived or died. Kamal had no obligation to anyone, for anything.

Snapping back to attention, Kamal then went back down the stairwell and returned to the main tower. He strode into the pool area and looked around. The old man with the gold chains hadn't returned from the beach yet, as he expected. Working his way around the tables again, he picked up a few glasses here and there, until he reached the table he'd gotten the key from.

Smoothly, he placed a dish on the table as if to steady his grip, but made sure to leave the key exactly where it was before. He then picked up the dish again, walked out through the side exit, and placed the dishes on a table in the hall, as he had done before.

Kamal made a line for the courtyard. As he walked through the resort, he felt as if every eye was on him. But not a single person said anything, and within a minute he was on his way back to the apartment.

• • • •

"Where did you . . . how much money is that?" Nicolette's eyes widened.

"About $9,000. Enough for us to live on for a few more months. Live *well*. And I got you a gift, too." Kamal showed her the diamond necklace.

"Where did you get all that? From the resort?"

"There's filthy-rich people everywhere. They leave their room keys, wallets, and everything just lying around. It's like stealing from a child."

"Won't they be angry?"

"Who are they going to tell? The police?" Kamal shook his head. "People are used to losing things when they vacation in another country. It's almost expected. Not worth the hassle to report it."

Nicolette frowned. "I think you should bring it back."

Kamal's eyes grew cold. "How do you expect us to survive, Nicolette?" His voice was fierce. "No one will hire us, coming from an orphanage. Besides, they have more money than they know what to do with."

Her face dropped, and she crossed her arms.

"Nicolette," he said softly, putting his hand on her shoulder. "You need to understand something. This world, all these people?" he continued, motioning at the city all around them. "They don't care if we live or die. *At all.* For us to survive, we're going to have to fend for ourselves."

Gradually, Nicolette's face softened, and she looked back up at Kamal. "I suppose that's true."

"You shouldn't feel bad about it. We deserve a chance at life, too."

She just nodded.

"In fact," Kamal insisted, "I want you to try it too, and see how easy it is."

• • • •

"I want you to just watch what I do," Kamal said. "I'm going to look for a table where they've left their keys. We wait for them to go down to the beach, then pass by and pretend to pick up dishes or dirty towels. We take the key to the room, clean out the safe, bring the keys back, then leave."

"That sounds pretty easy."

"Let's go." Kamal pointed and started walking.

Nicolette followed Kamal at a distance into the hotel lobby, making for the pool area. She used Kamal's pass to get in, while Kamal, in uniform, just strolled right past.

Nicolette thought the resort was beautiful, but she knew she couldn't take the time to enjoy it just yet. The pool area was crowded with people, so much so that it was difficult to keep an eye on Kamal. But through the crowd, she caught him single out a table where the resort guests had just stood up and were heading down to the beach.

Without any fuss, Kamal scooped up the dirty towels on the table and made his way back around to Nicolette. Without saying a word, he nodded towards the side entrance, and Nicolette watched him go through. She found a chair and sat, enjoying the view, and waiting for Kamal to return.

After about ten minutes, Kamal returned with fresh towels and placed them on the table he had attended earlier. He then approached Nicolette, smiled, and walked past her, back out of the courtyard.

Nicolette followed until they were both outside the gate, about two blocks away.

"How'd you do?" Nicolette asked.

"Here, look." He reached into his pockets and pulled out a stack of bills. "Not as much as last time, but plenty, all the same."

"What are we going to do with all this money?"

"We're going to live our lives," Kamal said. "We're going to live however we want. Don't you want that too?"

She nodded. "yes"

• • • •

Over the next few weeks, Kamal and Nicolette visited the resort every two or three days, with Kamal doing most of the work. At the end of a month, they had successfully pulled off six robberies—five by Kamal, one by Nicolette. Some of the returns weren't as profitable as their initial attempt, but overall, they had amassed a decent chunk of money.

This time, Nicolette had decided she wanted another shot at it.

"I think you can do it on your own," Kamal said.

Nicolette nodded. "I think I can. I feel confident."

"I'll stay here but don't you worry. You shouldn't run into any trouble."

Nicolette grabbed her resort uniform, changed, and headed out the door. Within thirty minutes, she was at the resort gates.

Nicolette made her way through the halls until she reached the pool area, which was still the easiest place to find unattended keys. The pool was crowded with people, as usual.

She walked through the clusters of people, smiling like one of the employees. She kept her eyes on the tables, though, and it wasn't long until she spotted a target.

The man looked younger than most of the businessmen there, maybe in his early forties. He was wearing a fancy robe and some reflective sunglasses. The young woman next to him was hanging out of a rather skimpy bikini. Nicolette watched them closely, until she saw them make their move to leave the pool and go down to the beach.

Just as she had done before, she swept around the edge of the room and cleaned up the table, making a note of where everything was. Nicolette then quickly left and walked back to the main resort's hotel area. Up the stairwell she went, finally stopping on the fifth floor.

The hallway was a little narrower and darker than the lower floors. Nicolette wondered if the rooms would be more cramped as well. But she found the key's door without any trouble, and quietly entered.

No one was inside, thankfully. She found the safe and just as Kamal had shown her, the small key unlocked it. Just as she was removing the money and things from the safe, there was a knock on the door.

Nicolette froze. Maybe it was just a guest who was at the wrong door. She hoped under her breath that they would just go away.

"Room Service," said a voice as the door unlatched and swung open. Nicolette stuffed the money into her pocket and stood.

"What do you think you're doing!?" The woman just stood there, blocking the door with her cart. Nicolette's mind raced for a way to get through, but she didn't think she could jump over the cart, and the lady was much larger than she was.

As room service started towards her, Nicolette let loose a blood-curdling scream. The violent noise jolted the woman backwards, and Nicolette made a beeline for the door.

Two men appeared from nowhere. The older one, the man Nicolette had stolen the key from. The other was a friend, or business partner. It didn't matter to Nicolette.

But as soon as she saw them, she froze. Something about the man looming in the doorway reminded Nicolette of Mr. Farouk. Maybe it was the look on his face, or the way he lunged at her.

She panicked. Couldn't move. In her mind, everything came to a complete standstill, and her stomach twisted in knots. Both men reached out and grabbed her by the arms. They had her. She struggled like a mouse in a snake's coiled grip.

The two men pulled her back into the room. Nicolette tried to scream, but nothing came out- her voice had vanished. They dragged her over to the bed, and Nicolette finally managed to scream again. As room service was about to leave to get security, there was a commotion in the hallway.

The woman shouted, then flew backwards and landed hard on the floor. And Kamal burst into the room.

It only took a second for Kamal to see Nicolette being held by the two men. Without hesitation, he jumped at them and threw his weight into a punch, which only partially landed. It was enough to get the man to let go of her, though.

"Run, Nicolette!" Kamal shouted as he started swinging his fists again.

As Nicolette dashed through the door and disappeared, the other man managed to grab a hold of Kamal's shirt and threw him to the ground. The guest he'd punched began raining down blows, yelling obscenities at Kamal.

"Disgusting, worthless street filth! I'll teach you not to steal from me!"

Blow after blow landed on Kamal's head. He saw lights. The other man kicked him square in the ribs, which took his breath away. Blood ran down his forehead and clouded his sight. He realized that if he didn't get up now, he never would again.

Hoping he'd bought Nicolette enough time, Kamal rolled into a crouch, reached into his front pocket, and pulled his knife.

"I'm going to wring your neck!" the older guest shouted and lunged again at Kamal. At the last second, Kamal dodged and sunk the knife into the man's belly as deep and as fast as he could. He could feel his wrist pop, most likely sprained from the wild flurry of punches he had thrown.

The man didn't drop immediately but staggered back. Kamal pulled his knife back, readying for another attack.

The younger man shouted and tried to grab Kamal, but the blade flicked back and forth, keeping him at bay. His arms spurted little streams of blood, and after a few seconds, he, too, fell back.

In the split second it took for them to catch their breath and get their bearings, Kamal sprinted for the door. He caught room service as she tottered down the hall with a well-placed kick to the back of her leg. She went sprawling.

Within seconds, he was skipping down the stairs two at a time, trying to wipe the blood from his face. His head pounded, his heart raced, and he could feel the bruises up and down his back with every breath.

He paused for a moment at the bottom floor, put his knife away, and took deep breaths to regain control of his breathing. Then he exited, walked around the far side of the complex, and headed towards the beach. Kamal figured they would expect him to go for the front gate, where there were more places to hide among the beachgoers.

Breaking into a slight jog, Kamal trotted on down to the edge of the water and jumped in, making sure to wash his face. The salt water stung, but it worked. For good measure, he removed his shirt and tried to blend in with all the other young men enjoying the surf. He swam along the shoreline until he reached an outcrop of rocks where he could return to land out of the view of the hotel.

It was a long, painful walk back to the apartment from there, but Kamal eventually made it. He opened the door and collapsed on the sofa.

Nicolette rushed towards him with a towel. She threw her arms around his neck, hugged him tight, and wept into his shoulder.

"I'm so sorry! I messed up everything!"

Kamal winced. "I'll be fine.don't worry I'm just glad you got away."

She looked at the bruises forming up and down Kamal's back, and held back a sob. "Because of me, this happened to you."

He shook his head. " I'm fighting for us," Kamal said as he gently wiped her tears. "I'll do whatever it takes to take care of you."

Nicolette tried to smile. Her eyes were still puffy and red from crying. "You saved me. You saved my life."

"Yes. But I . . . I shouldn't have had to. It's not your fault they came in," he said. "It's mine." Kamal paused long enough for his breathing to slow. "I can't risk that again."

For a few seconds, Nicolette just stared into Kamal's eyes. As their gaze locked, she sniffled and squeezed Kamal's hand. "I was so scared," she whispered.

"I know. And I'm sorry."

Another moment passed. Nicolette shook her head and wiped her face. "I guess I'm not very good at being a thief."

"Don't worry. Everything comes to an end," Kamal said. "Besides . . . we were never going to make real money stealing from hotel rooms."

"So what do you have in mind?" Nicolette asked.

"We need to wait a couple months . . . let things cool down. Then we'll figure something out, like we always do." Kamal smiled.

CHAPTER 4

DECEPTION

Kamal and Nicolette wandered down the street, through the tourist shopping district. Kamal liked to visit it, to watch tourists and think about how to blend in. Nicolette just liked looking in the shop windows.

"You see that?" Kamal pointed to a man exiting a jewelry store. "You can tell someone is rich by the way they dress. The way they act. The way they carry themselves," Kamal said to Nicolette. As they entered the next door upscale fashion boutique, she followed his eyes. "We need to look rich. Like we belong there." A display of evening gowns caught Kamal's eye. "Because we do."

After a couple of hours of choosing daytime and nighttime outfits and ensembles, Kamal decided it was time for lunch. Nicolette quietly agreed. As they left the shop, Kamal noticed a brand-new BMW M-series parked outside. It was a classy navy blue.

As they approached the sidewalk, Kamal stopped. "Why does he deserve to have a nice car and lots of money, and we don't?" Kamal got quiet. Then as usual, his mind worked through several scenarios.

"Nicolette, I have an idea. A way for us to finally get involved with the big money players."

"How?"

"We're going to need to steal a car. Not just any car, a nice one. We need better cover to pull off bigger scams. But it's going to take some work from both of us."

Nicolette, for once, looked excited about his idea. "You think we can do that?"

"I have no doubt."

• • • •

"What I need you to do," Kamal began, "is to look more like a spoiled, wealthy tourist."

Nicolette chuckled a little. "I'm not sure I understand. Do I not look spoiled enough?"

"What I mean is, you're going to need to start getting a tan. And if you want to look like them, you're going to have to get some exercise. All of those tourist girls are really fit and skinny."

"That sounds like a lot of work."

"It will be, but it needs to be convincing. Nobody is going to believe us if we don't look the part."

"Fair enough. I suppose we could get a membership at the health club a few blocks away."

"That's what I was thinking," Kamal agreed. "I'll go with you and show you what to do. You can get some nice makeup like they wear, maybe find some really good skin cream. And you're going to want to start brushing your hair daily, and taking care of yourself."

"Is all that really necessary?"

"Every little piece adds to the believability of our story. And besides," Kamal flashed a quick smile. "What's wrong with wanting to get in shape and taking care of ourselves?"

"I suppose so. When do we start?"

"Tomorrow. And while you're doing that, I'm going to be looking for a car."

• • • •

Kamal arrived at the BMW dealership. A dozen high-end cars were parked right in front. He wanted to watch some of the employees, but with nobody coming or going, it was going to take some time.

Eventually, he spotted a car salesman leaving for the day. As he walked to the front of the lot, a taxi pulled up, and the salesman and the taxi driver exchanged a few words. Then the salesman got in, and they started off.

Kamal followed from another cab for twenty minutes until they reached a sprawling apartment complex. The taxi parked, and both men got out and continued talking for a few minutes. Then with a wave, they both entered the complex. Kamal realized they must have known each other from being neighbors.

He started formulating a plan in his head, and as he did, Kamal thought this might be the best one yet. He was going to need a used car first, though—something to start with.

• • • •

A month later, Kamal had found a used car lot that had what he wanted—an older but still pretty white BMW. After a bit of haggling, he bought the car with cash, which the lot manager appreciated. Kamal then drove the car to a detail shop and had it completely cleaned, inside and out.

Next, he drove to a shopping mall a few miles away, and circled the parking lot until he spotted another white BMW of the same model. It could have been his car's twin. Kamal then stole the license plates from it, noting that they were from a different area of the country, which would be ideal.

Lastly, he headed back to the high-end tourist shops and found a store that did custom-tailored suits. He told them what he wanted, and about three hours later, he had a perfectly fitted suit, complete with new shoes and vest.

When he made it back to the apartment, Nicolette was there eating an afternoon snack. He could tell she had been getting lots of sun over the past few weeks as her hair was beginning to show highlighted streaks. Her skin had bronzed nicely.

"I'm going to need your help for this. But first I need to pay a visit to the arts district. I'll go tomorrow."

"Arts district?"

"Yes. We need an artist. An illustrator. We need a fake checkbook, but it has to look real. And we need one more thing—we're going to hire you a chauffeur."

• • • •

The next day, Kamal got dressed up in his tailored suit, while Nicolette put on a slinky cocktail dress and pulled her hair up. She completed the look with some dangly earrings and bright red lipstick.

"You look fantastic. That dress is perfect."

"Thank you!" Nicolette gave a little giggle and spun around.

"OK, are you ready? We're going to hire you a driver."

"Absolutely! How exciting!"

They jumped in the old BMW and before long reached the apartment complex where the taxi driver and the car salesman lived. Kamal parked on the street, close enough that he could see when the taxi left to bring the salesman to work.

As soon as the taxi left the parking lot, Kamal began following him through town. They eventually ended up in front of the dealership, where the salesman got out. The taxi then continued on into town to run his regular shift.

Around lunchtime, the taxi driver parked in a lot where several other taxis were parked. This must have been the usual lunch spot for taxi drivers to hang out. Kamal followed from a safe distance as the driver got out, walked up to a street vendor, got his lunch and a tea.

"Excuse me," Kamal finally called out.

"Yes?" the taxi driver said, caught off guard.

"I saw several taxi drivers come over here. I'm looking for someone interested in a new driving opportunity."

The driver raised an eyebrow. "What kind of opportunity?"

"I work for Mr. Farouk. You may know him. Know of him. The official."

"Yes. Who doesn't."

"Of course," Kamal said. "I am looking for someone to drive this young lady around while Mr. Farouk is on business. His wife knows all my regular drivers. I'm his chief of security, so I need someone from outside the organization. Does that sound like something you'd be interested in?"

The taxi driver barely hesitated. "Mr. Farouk! Yes, of course, assuming the pay is good."

"I'm willing to pay you ten times what you're charging for taxi fare now. Plus, you can use my car."

"Yes! That sounds perfect.

Kamal smiled. "Meet me here at the market tomorrow, and I'll take care of everything."

The taxi driver grinned ear to ear.

"Now if you'll excuse me, I have an errand to run for Mr. Farouk." Kamal bid his goodbyes and drove toward the arts district.

• • • •

Over the next two weeks, Nicolette had the driver chauffeur her all over town. They went to the spa, to the fitness center, and to every shopping center. She stayed busy, and each day, she would thank him when he dropped her off.

Eventually, it was time to make their move.

After a particularly normal morning, Nicolette tapped the driver on his shoulder.

"Mr. Farouk says he's wanting to buy me a new car."

The driver perked up. "Oh?"

"One of my friends just bought a nice one, and I'm wondering if you know where I can get one like it." She reached into her purse and pulled out a picture to show him.

"Hey, that's nice! I know a guy who sells luxury cars. He might have one like that in stock. Let me talk to him tonight and see."

"Perfect."

• • • •

A few days later, Kamal's white car pulled up to the new dealership. The taxi driver, now wearing a fancy uniform with epaulets and a hat, got out and opened the passenger door. Nicolette, wearing a silky, form-fitting gray dress and big sunglasses and her hair tied back in a tight bun, emerged and glided gracefully through the doors into the dealership showroom.

"I'll introduce you to my friend," the taxi driver said. "He will take care of you."

"Welcome," the driver's friend said warmly. He stepped around the front desk. "He told me what you're looking for," he nodded to the driver, "so let me show it to you."

Nicolette followed out a side door where the gray BMW 535 was parked.

"Beautiful," she said. "I'll take it."

"Excellent. So how would you like to pay, miss . . ."

"Janelle."

"Yes. Of course . . . Janelle. Will you be paying with cash or check? If you pay with a check, we require a ten percent down payment in cash."

"I have the down payment," she replied. "The rest will be covered with a check from Mr. Farouk."

The man's eyes widened. "Excellent. We've done business with him before. Let's get the paperwork started then, shall we? Our manager will take care of you. Right this way."

He motioned towards the manager's office, and Nicolette entered and greeted the manager. She pulled out her purse and a checkbook.

"I trust everyone took good care of you."

"Yes," she said. "Very."

"Good, good. So the BMW . . . that will be a $5,000 down payment, and the balance, $45,000, can be paid by check."

"Perfect." Nicolette counted out the money and laid it neatly on his desk. She then took a check from her checkbook, filled out the amount, and handed it to the manager.

"OK, this is already signed? That looks good. Is there anything else you need?"

"Just the car, thank you," Nicolette said.

"Excellent. Just fill out these papers, and we'll have you out the door in just a minute."

Nicolette filled out the papers with whatever she thought appropriate and handed them back to the manager. "Will that do?"

"Yes, thank you." He put the check, the cash, and all the paperwork into a manilla folder, and stood up. "Very well. Let's go get your car."

They walked outside to the lot where the attendant had pulled up the 535. Nicolette grinned. This really was easier than she thought.

The salesman reached inside, pulled the keys out and handed them to Nicolette. "Here you go, miss. This car comes with a full warranty, and . . ."

"That's good to know. I'll do my best not to break it."

Nicolette motioned to the taxi driver, who was still waiting nearby. "You can go home now. Just drop the car off. I'll drive myself the rest of the day. You have already been so helpful."

He nodded, gave a little bow, and then left.

With that, Nicolette slid into the car and quickly adjusted the seat forward. "This will do nicely."

"I do hope you enjoy it," the salesman said. "And make sure to tell him we appreciate his business."

Nicolette turned and pulled her sunglasses from her face, revealing her deep blue eyes. "Thanks for your help."

"My pleasure, Miss Janelle."

• • • •

"What do you mean, my 'girlfriend'?!"

"Sir, please," the dealership manager lowered his voice and quickly closed his office door. "All I know is, she said she was your girlfriend. She paid five thousand in cash and signed a check with your name on it."

"I didn't send anyone to buy a car!"

"But her driver. Doesn't he work for you? Your head of security?"

"My security is standing beside me right this very minute and knows nothing of this. You are lying."

"Mr. Farouk, I'm not lying, I swear to you."

Mr. Farouk said nothing.

"I'll make it right, sir. I promise you. I'll do whatever it takes. Sir, you do *not* have a girlfriend named Janelle. Is that right?"

"Yes!"

"Of course. And you do not have this secret driver. Is that right?"

"Yes."

"OK. I am sorry for disturbing you with this stupid mistake of ours."

Mr. Farouk hung up.

THE WOLF OF THE MIDDLE EAST

The manager took a deep breath, and picked up the phone again. "Hello, police?"

"How may I help you?"

The manager cleared his throat. "I'd like to report a theft—one of my employees and his friend managed to scam us out of a very expensive automobile."

"And you want us to arrest them?"

"Yes!" the manager blurted. "I want to see them in prison for a very long time!"

"Very well," the Lieutenant said. "We'll need a lot more information to be able to do that."

"Of course. Anything."

"Excellent. Please come by the station and fill out a report, and we'll send out a unit to pick them up as soon as possible."

· · · ·

"I think someone's following us." Nicolette scanned the mirrors, and then glanced at Kamal.

He snapped his attention from the road, and assessed the situation. "That black car? Looks like an undercover police cruiser?"

"Yeah."

"Dammit." Kamal gripped the wheel tightly and eased into the throttle. The stolen BMW slid through traffic like an eel, gliding effortlessly through gaps and spaces. It responded with every suggestion, every twitch of muscle, like an extension of Kamal's body.

"Do you think it's the cops?" Nicolette leaned back into her seat, bracing herself.

"No," Kamal said. "They'd have lit us up already if so. I'm thinking it's one of Farouk's men."

"Do you think they know who we are?"

"Don't think so," he answered tersely. "Think they just spotted the car."

For the next few minutes, Kamal worked his way through the streams of vacationers on the highway, trying to put as much space between them as possible. At every clearing, the BMW would pull hard. Every time he reached more traffic, the mystery car would catch back up.

"I don't think this is working," Kamal said. "I can still see them. We're going to have to get rid of the car somehow." He bit his lip. "We can't outrun them."

"Do you have any better ideas?"

Kamal scowled. "There's a few places we can lose them in the city, but it's going to be difficult."

At the next exit ramp, Kamal swung through the lanes and came to an intersection, where he promptly cut around under the highway overpass and headed back in the direction they had come from. It took a while to make sure, but eventually Kamal spotted the mystery black car again.

"Okay, good. They're back, but keeping distance." Kamal glanced behind him. "They have to know we've seen them by now."

"Keep going," Nicolette said. "I don't want to find out what they want."

Kamal pushed the limits of what the car could do, its engine roaring, until they reached the exit he was looking for. "There's one chance. If we can lose them through here, then we can ditch the car with a chop shop I know."

"I hope you're right."

Kamal just nodded. He whipped the BMW through an intersection, dove into a parking garage, and instead of circling around, headed straight through to the rear exit. From there, he headed straight for the heart of the city. He kept his head on a swivel, but the mysterious black car didn't materialize.

"I think we're good now," Kamal said. "But we've got to get rid of this thing. Grab your stuff, we're almost there."

A couple of minutes later, they turned into a large gated wall, with "Tony's Salvage" painted on the metal. Kamal pulled the BMW around the parking lot to the side of the shop, where it wasn't visible from the street.

As he stepped out of the car, Kamal was greeted by a beefy man in mechanic's coveralls. The patch on his chest proudly displayed the name "TONY".

"Hey, nice 5 series!" Tony said, grinning. "I love that color!"

"Thanks. I have a favor to ask, Tony."

"For you? Of course." Tony eyed the big BMW, and grinned. "You need me to buy this from you?"

"Afraid so. It's brand new, only a few hundred kilometers. We just can't keep it."

"I'll see what I can do. How much?"

"I want to get $30,000 for it. I know you can change the VIN, repaint it, then sell it as a different car for a lot more. I just need the cash right now. That's why I'm selling it to you for a lot less than it's worth."

"With a couple hundred kilometers?" Tony grinned again. "I think I can make that happen."

• • • •

Kamal and Nicolette stepped out of the airport shuttle and stood before a large hotel entrance. "We're going to use this place to lay low for a while," Kamal said. "Paris is a good place to get lost in the crowds."

"I can finally go shopping!" Nicolette beamed. "Maybe some sightseeing!"

"That's all good," Kamal replied. "But I have other plans while I'm here."

The next morning, Kamal headed for the nearest casino. He was ready, flush with cash, and in a mood to gamble.

When he entered the casino, Kamal's eyes had to adjust to the hazy, dim lighting. He took off his sunglasses, and spotting a poker table, pulled up a stool and began to play.

About ten hands in, he had doubled his money, and realized not only did he enjoy gambling, but was pretty skilled at it as well. Hand after hand, he increased the pot, and continued winning as people came and went.

After another hand, Kamal's phone buzzed in his pocket, prompting him to flip it open.

"Nicolette?" He paused, looked around, then continued speaking in Arabic. "Yes, I'm fine, I'm at the casino. I'll be back tonight. In fact. . ." Kamal smiled. "Can you meet me here? I need to ask you something. Excellent. I'll see you then."

After the conversation ended, Kamal put his phone back in his pocket and turned his attention back to the table, where he was being dealt another hand.

Hand after hand, Kamal came up winning, until he had amassed a sizable pile of chips in his corner. By this point, people had started noticing his winning streak,

After about an hour of playing, Kamal felt a pair of hands on his shoulder. Not a firm grip, though. The hands began massaging his shoulders, and turning, he saw a young woman, in a dress that barely covered anything, smiling back at him.

Kamal turned back to the card table, without saying a word.

"Pardon me," said a woman's voice from behind him.

Kamal turned again and was about to tell the woman he wasn't interested, but instead, the pretty girl in the revealing dress was standing, arms crossed.

"The man at the table over there would like to invite you to play at his table." She pointed to a dimly-lit spot, away from the main floor.

Kamal smiled. "Am I in trouble?"

"Not yet, no." The woman smiled and motioned for him to follow her.

As they approached the table, Kamal could see several businessmen smoking cigars and drinking brandy. In the center of the table was an older man, wearing a finely made white suit. He wore a thick gold ring and a Rolex. He exuded power the likes of which Kamal had never seen before.

Kamal stopped and raised an eyebrow. The girl in the dress nodded and disappeared into the crowd. He remained standing.

The man in the white suit looked up at him. "Young man, where are you from? Your accent sounds very familiar."

Kamal didn't flinch. "Where I'm from isn't important."

"You speak Arabic," the man said. "Are you Arab?"

"Lebanese. Why? Does that interest you?" Kamal countered. He was careful not to say anything that would offend.

"Come, sit," the man said. "You're a skilled player. I would like to play a few hands with you."

Before Kamal could sit, the man glanced at the other men around the table, and motioned with his head. Immediately, three of the men stood and left the table, leaving Kamal alone with the mysterious man and two of his bodyguards.

The dealer handed Kamal a hand of cards. The two men played quietly for a few minutes. Kamal could tell the man was sizing him up. Watching. Observing. Forming a first impression. For what?

"What do you do?" he finally asked Kamal.

"I make things happen," Kamal said.

"I'm a businessman. I look for opportunities to make money." The man puffed on his cigar and nodded. "And I can tell you've got the potential for making money."

Just then, someone emerged from the crowd and approached the table.

"Nicolette!" Kamal grinned. She was wearing a low-cut party dress and high heels. Kamal could sense all the eyes following her.

Without saying a word to anyone, Nicolette stepped around the table and whispered something in Kamal's ear. He nodded, and they exchanged a few quiet words. Then she straightened, turned, and left without a backwards glance.

"I apologize," Kamal said, turning back to the man at the table. "Now, what were you saying about making money?"

The man leaned forward. "My name is Al-Fahad, and I have a proposition for you, if you're interested."

"I'm always interested," Kamal replied.

"Good. I can see you also have good taste in women." Al-Fahad smiled, his eyes wrinkling around the edges. "I own a casino in Lebanon—in Beirut. The one next to the ocean resort."

"Oh, yes," Kamal nodded. "I know the one."

"We should continue this conversation there." He reached into his pocket and handed Kamal a business card. "I will be back there in two weeks. Call the casino and let them know you're coming. I'll be expecting you."

Kamal took the card and nodded.

· · · ·

"Nicolette, I'm not going to make it back to the hotel tonight," Kamal said. "Something's come up. I'll see you in the morning."

He hung up the phone and looked out over the beautiful Paris skyline. The wide balcony had several lounge chairs, offering a pristine view of the moonlit night sky. To the north, Kamal could see the Eiffel Tower.

Behind him, Kamal heard the sliding doors open as someone stepped out onto the balcony.

"Welcome," he said. "Come, enjoy the evening with me."

"That was the plan," said a soft voice. A beautiful young woman with flowing raven hair glided into view, wearing a very short party dress. "But first, let's handle business."

Kamal pointed to an envelope on the table nearby. The girl examined it, nodded, then tucked it away in her purse.

"I've always imagined Paris was beautiful, but seeing it lit up at dusk like this is just breathtaking."

The girl turned, hiked her dress up, and raised her leg up on the ledge, giving Kamal a full view of everything.

"Do you like what you see?"

"Yes, I like it, very much." Kamal grinned.

"I'm glad you like the view," she replied, stepping in front of him. She gave a little smile, turned, and slowly removed her dress, drawing closer to him as she did. She straddled Kamal and began unbuttoning his shirt slowly, working her way down, until she reached his belt.

"Keep going."

The girl smiled. "I intended to. I'm looking forward to you making me feel amazing."

"I can do more than that," Kamal whispered. "I can make you forget everything for a while."

She removed his pants and before long, they were intertwined, filling the night air with sounds of passion.

Kamal looked up into the night sky as his body shook with pleasure. It was almost something spiritual, supernatural. The entire world stood still, as he rode wave after wave of ecstasy. They did not return indoors until the first light of morning.

At sunrise, when passions were waning, Kamal fell into the window-facing lounge chair and exhaled deeply. He felt at peace. For a moment.

Then he imagined Nicolette.

The moment abruptly ended.

CHAPTER 5

RUTHLESS

Kamal took one look at the entrance to the casino and smiled. The building was both elegant and dilapidated. He knew what lay inside. And he was ready. Al-Fahad had invited him to his home casino in Lebanon, so when they had finished their trip to Paris, he made sure to accept the invitation.

Kamal slowly made his way through the entryway, past rows and rows of slot machines, pausing in the middle of the main game floor. The clattering of roulette wheels and the shouts of dealers filled the air as gamblers roamed the room.

"Kamal? Welcome!"

Kamal turned his head to see a man in a white suit walking toward him with his arms extended, flanked by two larger men dressed in black.

Kamal nodded. "Hello, Al-Fahad."

"Come, sit. Let's talk." Al-Fahad motioned towards a booth in the corner, waiting for Kamal to walk ahead of him.

Kamal nodded once, walked toward the booth, and slid into a seat. Al-Fahad sat across from him, but the two larger men remained standing.

Al-Fahad smiled as he produced a cigarette and lighter from his pocket. He lit the cigarette, took a long, slow draw, and clacked the lighter shut again. "Kamal, I see you accepted my invitation." He tucked the lighter back into his pocket.

"Yes. It would have been rude not to." Kamal agreed.

"True. I'm in need of an industrious young man like yourself."

Kamal nodded again. "Of course. What's the job?"

Al-Fahad smiled widely. "We're trying to run a business that gives people what they want— what they *need*— to run their *own* businesses. But we've run into some obstacles."

"And how can I help?" Kamal asked.

"When we receive shipments from other countries, it's common for the port authorities to . . . overextend their responsibilities. And very often, they decide to keep things that don't belong to them." Al-Fahad leaned forward. "Things that people have paid for. Things that those business owners are relying on to feed their families with."

"I see."

Al-Fahad took another drag from his cigarette. "Now for us to properly receive these shipments, they require approval. We need signatures from very important people. And I know you can help us get these signatures."

Kamal glanced at one of the spinning roulette wheels as he masterminded the best way to manipulate the victim to get what he wanted.

"I can see you are deep in thought, and rightfully so," Al-Fahad continued. "I'll just say this: I would never ask you to hurt anyone or steal anything. We simply need some cooperation, and you look like someone who can make that happen." Al-Fahad once more brought his cigarette to his lips. "We would, of course, pay you quite well for your services"

Kamal smiled. No matter how dangerous the proposition was, Kamal was always up for the challenge—and the reward. This kind of deal was what he lived for, and Al-Fahad's connections to the black market were second to none.

"I understand," Kamal replied. "I'll get the job done."

• • • •

Kamal and Nicolette were outside a deli on the corner near their apartment complex. The duo entered, scanned the room, and found a seat. Lunch rush would begin shortly. Sparse customers offered privacy while they ate.

"We've been given a job to do," Kamal began. "It requires your help."

"Anything, Kamal. Of course," Nicolette said.

"I need your help trying to convince someone to sign some paperwork for Al-Fahad."

"What's my role?"

"Just be yourself, like usual. With . . . a few modifications."

"Who's the target?"

Kamal cleared his throat. "The Minister of Commerce. But he's clean."

"How clean?"

"So clean that money isn't enough."

"So what's the angle?"

"I have a plan. . . and I know how we can convince him to sign the papers." He paused, then added quietly, "Not a lot will be hurt in the process."

Nicolette relaxed slightly, but her eyes were narrowed. "What could possibly motivate him?"

"I've done some research. I've figured out his weakness."

"And?" Nicolette waited.

"He's very charitable. He donates money to the poor, he attends mosque regularly, and he's a family man. You're right, we can't blackmail him, we can't bribe him with money or power . . . but I think he'll be more inclined to listen to a kinder, more innocent face than mine. We can leverage his desire to help people." Kamal smiled. "His weakness is that *he's a good man.*"

Nicolette sat back and folded her arms across her chest.

"I've been following him for a month now," Kamal continued. "I know who he talks to. I know when he arrives at work and when he leaves. I know when he goes to the store, when his children leave school, where his favorite restaurants are. In fact," Kamal looked around and lowered his voice, "I've written down every single thing he does. His entire life is right here." He pulled a folded paper out of his jacket pocket.

Nicolette took a long stare at the old paper menu. "OK, you're right. That might be useful."

"There's a lot of money in it for us this time," Kamal added. "More than double the last job."

"Let's do it. What's the plan?"

Kamal reached into his jacket pocket and pulled out a pair of dark sunglasses—and a folded-up white cane. "For starters, you'll need these."

• • • •

The State Commerce building was constantly bustling with activity—the foot traffic never stopped.

Nicolette sat alone on a bench in the main hallway, watching from behind the dark lenses. She held a black notebook with Braille writing on the cover in her lap. Her cane leaned against the bench beside her.

After an hour had passed, Nicolette spotted him: the Minister of Commerce. He was a shorter, slightly overweight man in his mid-fifties, but he looked polished and clean.

Nicolette stood, grabbed the cane, and with quick tapping motions, flicked it back and forth on the ground in front of her. As she headed for the elevator, she carefully paced her steps so that she would reach it at the same time as the Minister. As they converged, she hesitated for just a second, until the Minister put his finger on the elevator button. She reached out as if to press the same button, but put her hand on his instead.

"Oh!" She gasped. "I'm sorry!"

"No, it's fine, my apologies," said the Minister of Commerce. "Are you going up?"

"Yes, please," she replied. "I'm looking for someone." As the doors opened, she stepped carefully into the elevator.

"Who are you looking for?" he inquired, following her inside. "I might know where they work."

"I was told to come see Omar Najar, the minister of commerce," she replied softly. "Do you happen to know him?"

"How can I help you? I'm Omar."

"Oh!" Nicolette smiled. "I was afraid it would be hard to find you."

"Come," Omar said as the elevator doors opened. "Let's go to my office."

Nicolette nodded. "Which way?"

"Here, let me take your arm."

Omar led her gently by the elbow through a series of turns to a large wooden door with a small window. "Here we are. Have a seat here." He put her hand on a chair in front of his desk.

Nicolette reached out and felt the desk's corner as she sat down, still holding the black notebook.

"Now, miss . . . I'm sorry, I didn't catch your name."

"Nicolette," she replied with a shy smile. "My name is Nicolette."

"Yes, Miss Nicolette." Omar cleared his throat and his voice took on a more formal tone. "So you were told to come see me. What can I help you with?"

"My brother has taken care of me for years, but recently, he's. . ." Her face fell. "He's gotten into some trouble." She pulled out some folded paperwork from her notebook and said, "All I know is that for him to be forgiven, he needs these papers signed."

Omar took the papers and looked them over. "Oh, I see. I—um, how do I say this?" he stammered. "I've seen these problems with shipments before. Quite often, actually."

Nicolette nodded. "Yes? So can you help me?"

"Well, I . . . I'm not sure how I can help you." The Minister of Commerce shook his head. "You're asking me to sign something I cannot."

Nicolette dropped her head. "I . . . I don't understand." She sniffed, and when she spoke, her voice wavered. "Is there something wrong?"

He sighed. "These sorts of imports are illegal."

"I don't know what my brother is doing or what his shipment is. I just know I need my brother in my life. If this shipment doesn't go through, he won't be able to come around again."

"No, that would be illegal. I am a man who lives by his morals." Omar sat back and closed his eyes. "I'm sorry I cannot help you, Miss Nicolette."

Quietly, Nicolette began to sob. Omar tried to soothe her. "Oh Miss Nicolette, I am so very sorry."

Nicolette wiped away fake tears and shook her head.

"Look, I understand," said Omar. "I'm sure there's some other way to help your brother."

"I am sorry for wasting your time," Nicolette choked out. She sniffled again. "I should have known better." She held out her hand, and it shook a bit.

"I really am very sorry. I wish I could help you."

Nicolette nodded, and with an innocent voice, said, "Thank you for your time, Mr. Najar."

Omar watched as she grabbed her cane and walked out the door. For a moment, he stood staring after her. When he finally looked down, he saw her black notebook on the chair.

• • • •

The sun shone brightly through the blossoming trees lining the park. It was early evening and several families were out enjoying themselves. Sounds of children playing and laughing filled the air.

Omar Najar stood next to a tree with a camera around his neck, watching the rays of light slowly drift towards the horizon. Evening was his favorite time to photograph. It was one of the few hobbies he was able to indulge in, and he loved taking pictures for his wife and children to enjoy. He swept his viewfinder across the park, looking for a game of some sort, or perhaps a flying kite for a nice photograph. Then he froze.

The blind woman he'd met yesterday was sitting on a park bench just a stone's throw away.

He blinked. Yes, it was most definitely the same woman. He focused his camera on her face, taken by how beautiful she was. "What a shame," he muttered to himself, "that she's blind and will never know how pretty she is." Carefully, he began to snap pictures of Nicolette. Click. Click-click. Click.

As he played back their first meeting in his mind, he suddenly remembered about the notebook she had left behind in his office.

Omar straightened himself, shouldered his camera, and approached Nicolette.

"Excuse me," he called. "It's me, Omar Najar. Do you remember me?"

"Mr. Najar?" She pulled back slightly.

Omar approached the park bench, relief washing over him. "It is you! Miss Nicolette, you came to my office the other day. I thought I recognized you."

"You have a good memory," she said softly.

"Thank you. It's good to see you." Omar looked across the park. "I love coming here in the evenings. The sunsets here are glorious."

"Look, Mr. Najar, about that visit . . . "

"Please, call me Omar."

"Mr. Omar, again, I'm sorry . . . "

"Ah, yes, about that," he said. "I wanted to apologize."

Nicolette stopped cold. " I understand if you couldn't . . . "

"You left your notebook in my office," he interrupted. "I'm sorry, but it didn't have an address on it, so I just held on to it. I wasn't sure what to do." He paused for a moment, then added, "I'm working this week, but I can meet you this weekend and bring it to you. Would that be OK?"

"Yes," Nicolette beamed with relief. "That book is very important to me. Should I meet you here?"

"Yes, of course," Omar said. "Do you come to the park often?"

Nicolette shrugged. "I enjoy the sounds of children playing. I would love to have a family like that." She lowered her head. "Maybe someday."

"I like to take photographs of the people and the flowers, but especially the sunsets," Omar said.

"Oh," she said sadly. "What are the sunsets like? Can you describe it to me?"

"It's . . . like a warm, beautiful blanket of colors spread across the sky and the land," he said. "The light changes everything. It makes things look softer." He turned back to her and smiled. "The way it highlights your hair is very beautiful. Forgive me, I had to capture it on film."

Nicolette's brow furrowed. "You took pictures of me? But why would you take pictures of me if I can't see them?"

Omar swallowed hard. "If you knew how beautiful you are, you wouldn't ask me that."

Nicolette stood, turned, and with her cane, began walking away.

"Wait!" Omar called. "What are you doing this weekend?"

Nicolette stopped. "I don't have any plans," she said. "I have no one to spend weekends with."

"Is there no one else to take care of you?" Omar asked. "To at least . . . help with things?"

"Not really," she replied. "I've had to find ways to manage things, and without my brother's help getting things done, it's been difficult."

Omar's heart sank. After a few seconds, he blurted out, "How about I show you around the park on Saturday? There's an ice cream stand on the other side. Do you like ice cream?"

"Of course. Who doesn't? But you don't have to."

"No, really," Omar said. "Just meet me here at five, and I'll tell you all about sunsets, and bring you your notebook."

"OK," she said with a smile. "I'll be here." She tilted her head, and added, "I can tell it's getting late because of the chill in the air. I should be going home."

"Will you be OK going home in the dark?" Omar said, and then slapped his forehead, realizing what he'd said.

Nicolette laughed. "It makes no difference to me! Until Saturday, then."

"Yes, Saturday. Goodnight, Nicolette."

"Goodnight, Omar." And Nicolette made her way quickly down the path toward the park's entrance. She kept walking around a corner, where a car was parked and waiting out of sight. Nicolette stepped inside.

"Did he take your photograph?" Kamal asked after she shut the door.

"Yes," Nicolette said. "He couldn't keep his eyes off me."

"So, same plan this weekend?"

"Yes. He's going to describe sunsets for me." Nicolette rolled her eyes and laughed.

"How much longer do you think this will take?" Nicolette stared impatiently out the car window. "If it's possible, I think he's taking too much of an interest in me."

"That's what we want," Kamal insisted as he pulled away from the curb. "You aren't asking him to do any of this. It's his decision."

"He has children!" said Nicolette. "I don't want them to go through any trouble."

"He also has a luxurious life and makes lots of money for the government. We're not trying to ruin him." Kamal paused, then sighed. "I just need his signature."

"I know." Nicolette shook her head.

"We just need to be patient. I know it's taking longer than we'd hoped. But I really think this will work." Kamal smiled. "It'll all be over soon and we'll enjoy the fruits of our labor."

"I know." Nicolette smiled. "Do you think he'll sign the papers soon?"

"I'm counting on it."

• • • •

"Here, these belong to you"

Nicolette sat on the same park bench. She smiled and turned her head toward the familiar voice. "Hello, Omar. Is it the notebook?"

"Yes." He laid Nicolette's notebook gently into her lap. "You left it in my office that day, remember?."

"Oh!" She sat upright, touching the notebook's cover with her hands. "Thank you for returning it!"

Omar cleared his throat and spoke softly. "So, who wrote those words inside, about people not wanting to help anyone anymore? And 'I hope someone can tell me if it's worth it to look outside into the world, or keep my eyes shut'?"

Nicolette inhaled sharply. "You read it?"

"I had to. I wanted to know more about you."

"But it's my personal journal." Nicolette frowned slightly. "My brother wrote that for me. My hand gets tired from the Braille, and he transcribes my thoughts for me sometimes."

"Again," Omar said, "I meant no harm. But your words impacted me. I wanted you to know, not everyone in the world is as bad as you think."

An awkward silence hung in the air.

"It certainly feels that way sometimes," Nicolette sighed.

"I understand how someone like you could feel that way," Omar said. "But not everyone is consumed with self-interest."

THE WOLF OF THE MIDDLE EAST

"I don't see many people willing to help others. At least, not selflessly. Not without something in return."

"There are very few," Omar admitted.

"I think you are a man with a good heart," Nicolette said quietly. "I'm sure you see all sorts of bad things, and yet somehow you remain positive."

"Thank you. I . . . I try my best to help others. Sometimes, it's not so easy."

"I agree." Nicolette nodded.

"I said I would bring you around the park and describe the sunset. Are you still okay with that?"

"Yes," Nicolette said with a nod. "Absolutely."

As the late afternoon's intense sunshine waned, Omar led Nicolette around the park's paved paths, pausing to describe the sights for her. It took nearly twenty minutes, but eventually they stopped at a small white cart, just as they were about to close.

"Please!" pleaded Omar, "Can we get just two scoops of ice cream?"

With a reluctant stare, the vendor obliged, and handed them two cones.

"You have to be careful eating these," Omar explained. "I can help you if you like."

Nicolette carefully raised the treat to her mouth and took a taste. "*Mmm.*" She smiled and licked her lips. "This is delicious! I never get treats like these!"

"I imagine you've lived a very difficult life," Omar said. "And I wanted to make it a bit brighter."

"Thank you so much," Nicolette gushed. "With my brother gone, it's been so lonely." She inhaled deeply. As she let out her breath, her lip trembled. "I'm so thankful I met you, Omar," she said softly, her voice quivering.

"Please don't cry!" Omar couldn't stand to see her tears. "Look, your ice cream is about to drip! Quickly, finish it, before it makes a mess!"

Nicolette laughed, and as they finished their dessert, Omar felt something that he hadn't felt in a long time.

Omar looked away for a moment. "Nicolette, do you trust me?"

"I'm. . . not sure what you mean," she said slowly. "You've been so kind to me."

"Ah, I'm only doing what any good person would do." Omar thought for a moment. "In fact, is there anything else I can do for you?"

Nicolette frowned. "I couldn't ask you to. . ."

"Anything," insisted. "Just name it."

"I am running out of meals to eat." She lowered her head. "I feel so embarrassed just saying it, but I don't have any money to go shopping. My brother used to take care of that for me."

Omar's eyes softened. "Tell you what, I'll bring you some food this week."

"I couldn't possibly accept!"

"No, it'll be no bother whatsoever." Omar placed his hand on her shoulder. "You shouldn't have to suffer because of what your brother did."

"Thank you!" Nicolette smiled widely and wiped away a tear from behind her shades. "No one has been this kind to me before."

"Would you be upset if I brought you home?" Omar looked concerned. "I hate the thought that there's no one to walk you home."

Nicolette flashed a kind smile. "I would appreciate that."

Omar beamed. Then a thought popped into his head. "Would you meet me here again next weekend? I want to show you something."

"Yes, for sure!"

Omar just smiled.

• • • •

A taxi pulled up next to the curb, and Omar stepped out. Reaching back into the car, he carefully helped Nicolette onto the sidewalk. The cry of seagulls filled the air with a background of ocean waves.

"I wanted to surprise you," Omar said. "When was the last time you were at the beach?"

Nicolette gasped. "Oh, not since I was a child!" Breathing deeply, she smiled. "I can smell the salt in the air."

Omar took Nicolette by the arm and led her past the small shops lining the walkway to a path leading down to a sandy beach.

"Why would you bring me here?" Nicolette asked. "I mean, it's lovely, but I don't understand. . ."

"I want you to feel the beauty of the world, not be consumed with the darkness around you," he replied. "Life can be filled with goodness and wonder, but only if you look for it."

Nicolette slipped off her shoes, feeling the sand beneath her feet.

"Do you like it?" Omar asked hesitantly. "It's wonderful," she breathed.

"We can stay as long as you like," Omar said. "I'm just glad you like it." Omar looked at Nicolette in awe. Her smile, the way the wind blew her hair, the way she walked through the sand—everything about her was graceful. And yet, he was torn. For Omar to save her meant risking great sacrifice. But the more time he spent with her, the more his resolve wavered.

Nicolette smiled and nodded. "Yes, this truly was a surprise!"

"I'm glad we saw each other again that evening," Omar said, then turned red as he realized his blunder. "I'm so sorry, I mean—"

Nicolette laughed. "It's OK. I know what you meant." Then she added, "Me, too."

"I have one more thing for you," Omar said. "I didn't want to give this to you at first because it goes against my morals. But I wouldn't be a good person to refuse to help a pure hearted woman like you who is in trouble."

Reaching into his pocket, Omar produced a trifold of papers and put them in Nicolette's hands. "These are the papers your brother requested. It was the least I could do."

Nicolette feigned shock, but underneath her dark shades, she knew it—*I've got him*. Months of work were finally validated. Now she just had to find a way out.

"Thank you. Thank you!" Nicolette beamed, cried, and laughed all at once. She threw her arms around Omar's neck and hugged him tightly. "How can I ever repay you?"

"Since I've known you, Nicolette, you have been an inspiration to me.your beauty, your sincerity . . . I'm glad I met you, because you have changed my life for the better."

"How so?" Nicolette smiled innocently.

"I want to be with you," he declared. "I've realized that you make me happy in a way that no one else could. I want to marry you, Nicolette."

"But you're married! You have a family, kids, a life. Don't throw it all away for . . . for me!"

"I've already made up my mind."

• • • •

"I've got to get out of this place for a while," Nicolette said tersely. "This is just too much heat for me right now."

"I understand," Kamal said. "He didn't try anything suspicious, did he?"

"No, no, not at all," she replied. "He's exactly like you said he would be. But to ruin his life and try to marry me!"

"You are quite the actor." Kamal grinned. "So what did you do?"

"I played his heart," she said. "I told him I needed some time. And that a blind girl could never take care of him the way his own wife did. That I didn't deserve him."

"But did you turn down the proposal?" Kamal asked.

"No," Nicolette said. "Now he just wants me more."

"Well then." Kamal held out his hand. "Did you bring the forms?"

"Yes, I have them right here." Nicolette handed over a manilla folder. "I'm glad it's done. Now we can take that holiday in Monaco I've been waiting for."

"I just have to deliver these to Al-Fahad and deposit the money," Kamal said. "Then we can relax once we get to the villa,"

"Good," Nicolette said. "I can't wait till we get there. Is there anything I should bring?"

"I don't think you'll have to worry about packing," Kamal said with a wry grin. "I'll take care of everything."

• • • •

"Thank you," Omar said curtly as the taxi pulled away. He turned, and seeing the squat apartment complex, his hopes rose. Grasping a bouquet of flowers tightly, he made his way to the second floor and scanned each doorway until he eyed Apartment 213.

As he approached, he noticed an unusual noise at first. Not trusting his ears, he drew closer, until he could hear the sound quite clearly, coming from Nicolette's apartment.

It was the unmistakable sound of two people having vigorous, rather vocal, sex.

Taken aback, Omar promptly stepped to the door and pounded on it with his fist. "Nicolette, are you there? Are you all right?" His heart raced as his mind went through horrific, imaginary scenarios.

The ruckus ceased, and seconds later, the door was flung open from inside. In the doorway—naked—Kamal, still breathing heavily.

Omar shook his head. He tried to form words, but his heart pounded even harder, as he eyed Kamal up and down with a scowl.

Omar lunged forward, as if to push his way past Kamal, but he was no match for Kamal's younger, stronger physique. Harder and harder, Omar's heart pounded in his chest. He could feel it in his neck, his temples, his face, like they were about to burst.

A brief tussle ensued, but Omar shortly ran out of steam, and hard as he tried, he couldn't overpower Kamal in any way.

"You should go home, old man," Kamal said hotly. "You have no business here."

Omar managed to stand with some effort, but could only stand there as his heart continued to pound incessantly.

"Who's there?" came a woman's voice from inside the apartment. But the voice was not Nicolette's. A juvenile, also naked, appeared next to Kamal, and through hazy vision, Omar could see that her face wasn't Nicolette's either.

"Nobody," Kamal spat. "Go get dressed, we're leaving."

"I don't—I don't understand," Omar stuttered. And then through the doorway, on an end table, he saw them.

Nicolette's dark sunglasses sat, neatly folded, on top of the paperwork containing his signature. Her cane was leaning against the wall next to the table.

And it was then that Omar Najar realized he had made a horrible mistake. With a shout, he lunged for the papers. The only way to save his reputation was to tear them up.

Just as he was close enough to grab them, there was a blur of motion as Nicolette snatched the papers right out from under his fingers.

"I can't let you do that, Omar." She stood there staring him down, and for the first time, Omar saw her piercing eyes. Nicolette's unwavering gaze was cold.

Omar's world spun as his vision became more and more blurry. His hands clenched into fists. "No!" he gasped. "No!"

Kamal, still naked, grabbed Omar around the waist and pulled him back towards the front door. Despite struggling, Omar couldn't break free of Kamal's grip. Finally, Kamal wheeled him around and gave him a shove through the door.

Omar stumbled a few steps until his foot caught on the welcome mat, making him lunge forward. His arms flailed, but found nothing to catch himself with. He began tumbling, tumbling, down the stairs.

He slammed into the ground like so much dead weight. There was a loud crunch as he landed, and excruciating pain shot through his body like lightning. The last thing Omar remembered before blacking out was Kamal's voice calling for an ambulance.

• • • •

"I received the paperwork intact. A portion of the money has been deposited in your bank account, as you requested. You've done well, as I expected."

Kamal smiled. He stood next to a public pay phone, holding a small suitcase in one hand, and the phone receiver in the other. "Thank you, Al-Fahad. Everything went smoothly."

"That's not what I heard!" Al-Fahad laughed. "My friend, I told you it wasn't necessary to hurt anyone."

Yes, about that . . ." Kamal shook his head. "That actually was an accident. The Minister fell down the stairs, broke his leg, and could have dislocated his shoulder . . ."

"Sure, sure," Al-Fahad said. More laughter roared. "It was on the news that he retired from his government position from his hospital bed!"

"Yeah, that was unfortunate," Kamal said with a chuckle. "But who knows, maybe he will find what he's looking for. Maybe it was for the best."

Al-Fahad said, still laughing. "All it takes is one bad decision."

CHAPTER 6

ANNIHILATION

Kamal snapped open the latches on the leather briefcase and raised the lid. For a moment, he thought about all the things he could buy with that much money. More importantly, he knew what it was really worth—freedom.

"As we agreed, here is your payment." Across the table, Al-Fahad smiled beneath the brim of his wide hat. "I must say, my friend, you came through on your promise."

Kamal closed the briefcase and nodded. "It was my pleasure."

"Good. Very good. Our business associates appreciated your help getting the papers signed."

With nothing more, Kamal readied to leave. He stared past his client at the reflection in one of the long windows. Kamal's green eyes stared back at him, his dark hair fell just below his sharp, freshly shaved jaw, and his gray suit drew attention to his strong shoulders.

"Wait." Al-Fahad raised a hand. "There's something else."

"Oh?"

"Since you've been so helpful, I have another proposition."

"Go on."

"This will be much more challenging. Do you think you and your woman can pull it off?"

"I am always confident," Kamal said. "But I like details."

"Are you familiar with private art collections? Paintings?"

"I can learn. What do you need me to do?"

"I have a friend. A collector. And he has been trying to get a particular painting for years."

"Why hasn't he?"

"The beauty belongs to an appraiser named Sophia, a very obsessive woman. A recluse. She herself has a large collection of paintings. But no matter how much was offered, she has refused to sell this particular painting. We don't know why."

"What do you want me to do?"

"I want you to acquire that painting . . . by any means necessary."

"I see." Kamal pressed his fingertips together as he thought it over. "I'm going to need to do some research."

"Good. My contact was willing to pay the appraiser handsomely for it, so money is no object. Just let us know what you need."

"I will."

"Sophia Hadad is a professional artist and appraiser, so she's very familiar with spotting fakes. She will be difficult to convince, but I'm confident you will do what it takes." Al-Fahad patted the briefcase. "Your track record speaks well of you."

"It does."

Al-Fahad slid a folder across the table. "I thought you might agree—and that you would accept. Here is some information about the painting and the appraiser. There's a list of everything in her collection, everything she's bid on, and everything she's sold. Contact me if you need anything."

"I will." Kamal stood.

"Oh, and Kamal? We just need the one painting. If you happen to take possession of more artwork than that, do with it as you wish."

"Understood."

• • • •

That night as Kamal looked through the portfolio over and over, something began to be noticeable. Almost every painting in this collector's possession were portraits or studies of women. Some looked innocent, some laughed, some were overcome by background landscapes. Some appeared mysterious, even lonely or misunderstood. But every single painting had a beautiful woman in it somewhere.

The painting they were concerned with specifically was a wonderful scene of a young woman in a blue satin velvet dress, dancing. Her face was serene, but sad. Her eyes looked like they would come right through the canvas and stare into your soul.

Why would a female art collector have a collection almost entirely of women? Kamal went back through the photos, hoping to spot some other connection. Then it struck him: They're all facets of the same woman—the ideal woman. Kamal slapped the table. *Of course! She won't sell that painting because it reminds her of the perfect woman.*

• • • •

"How may I help you?"

Kamal smiled at the woman behind the counter. "I'd like to pull records for someone, please."

"What's the name?"

"Sophia Hadad."

The woman tapped on her computer's keyboard, then frowned. "I found that name, but I don't see anything. . ." she paused for a second. "Is that her maiden name, or married name?"

"Of course!" Kamal shook his head. "It's probably under her married name."

"Ah, yes." She tapped some more, then raised an eyebrow. "Which one?"

Kamal thought hard. "I'd like to see them all."

"I see. . ." the woman sighed. "There's a processing fee for printed records."

Kamal grinned and pulled out his wallet. "Name your price."

Thirty minutes later, Kamal was sitting at a table in a bistro, looking through a stack of photocopied records. There were things like changes of address, property tax forms, and marriage documents, which was surprising.

But the biggest thing that surprised Kamal wasn't that Sophia had been married. It was that she'd been married—and divorced—twice. He read through the court filings, and noticed the dates were quite a few years apart. In fact, both divorce proceedings had dragged on for more than 3 years each. Skimming the court transcriptions, he could see that both cases had settled arbitration for large sums of money, and no children were mentioned anywhere.

Considering how unusual it was for a divorce to go through, it was even more surprising that Sophia had managed to come out so well. There was something strange about it, but Kamal couldn't quite put his finger on it. There was one more place he needed to go.

• • • •

The art gallery was brightly lit, and quiet noises filled the room as people milled about admiring the paintings and sculptures. Each archway led into another room of neat displays and observation benches. There were soft lights aimed at each piece, giving the whole place a cozy glow. The art was interesting, but Kamal wasn't there to appreciate paintings. He took his time going around the rooms, keeping his eyes on everyone who looked like more than a casual observer. There were a handful of wealthy businessmen there, along with some pretentious collectors.

Kamal wore a sharp suit to fit in among the high-end crowd. He made his way through the crowd of people until he caught sight of his target: Sophia Hadad. She stood a few inches taller than other women nearby. And unlike the others, who wore colorful dresses and skirts, Sophia sported a black and white jumpsuit pantsuit. Her black hair laid flat down her back. But even though her appearance seemed to not draw attention, her eyes were piercing. There was something about the way she moved that was magnetic. Her aura, for lack of a better word, seemed to effortlessly draw people to her.

Sophia was surrounded by a group of businessmen asking her questions about her art collection. From what Kamal could see, she socialized effortlessly, handling each question with aplomb. He stayed to the side, managing to catch a bit of the conversation.

"Thank you. I've tried to capture the essence of femininity with my pieces." Sophia spoke with a firm conviction that impressed Kamal.

"Have you considered offering commissioned art?"

"No," Sophia replied. "I create what I am inspired by. If others are, too, then they buy it. I enjoy the freedom of painting and collecting only what I want."

"Would you be interested in discussing future projects, say, tomorrow night? Over dinner?" One of the younger businessmen, fairly handsome and dressed very sharply, flashed her a grin.

"No." Her tone was firm but not harsh. "That's what I'm here today for. Are there any other questions?"

"Excuse me."

Sophia turned and a young woman stepped forward from behind her.

"Yes?" Sophia's voice softened instantly.

The young woman looked a bit nervous. "I was wondering if you could tell me who your favorite artists are. I'm really impressed with your work."

"Yes, of course," Sophia said, her eyes softening. "One of my favorites is right over here. Please, I'd love to show it to you." Sophia gently wrapped her arm around the girl's waist and led her away.

Something about the way Sophia spoke and carried herself clicked in his mind. Kamal smiled and turned to head for the entrance. He had seen enough.

• • • •

"Nicolette!"

"Yes?"

Kamal looked up from where he sat. A young woman with long, flowing dark hair, baby blue eyes, and a wide smile turned and walked over to the table. A casual observer might have mistaken her face for that of a teenager's, but her eyes radiated an intensity beyond her years. Her short shorts and v-neck shirt revealed long muscular legs and ample cleavage. She leaned over the papers spread across the table, giving Kamal a clear view of pretty much everything. Her thighs drew his eyes astray, until her voice snapped him out of his stare.

"What is all this?"

Kamal pointed to the papers. "This is what we're going after." Nicolette began looking through the photographs of paintings, and after a moment, she smiled.

"He has a thing for beautiful girls, does he?"

"They always do." Kamal nodded. "Except it's not a 'he.' How do you feel about playing that part?"

Nicolette smiled and raised an eyebrow. "Oh? What's the plan?"

Kamal paused. "I want you to make her fall in love with you."

"That's easy. Making people fall for me is my thing."

• • • •

"This mansion looks beautiful," Nicolette said.

"Yes. But this is still going to require some work. We've got a truck coming later today with furniture." Kamal looked around the large foyer and nodded. The marble floor was inlaid with decorative tile mosaics, and each wall had alcoves to be filled with sculpture or paintings. An enormous crystal chandelier made everything come alive with a warm glow.

"So what exactly is the story with this collector? How is renting a mansion going to get us that painting?"

Kamal pointed to the empty alcoves. "We're going to fill the place with art pieces she'll appreciate. You're going to play the part of a widow who wants to appraise the art and draw in her interest." Kamal grinned. "I've even got a special piece made, just for her."

"Are you sure that'll work?"

"Have I ever steered you wrong?"

"Of course not." Nicolette gave a look that said everything.

"OK. Once we get everything moved in, I want you to contact this collector, and ask if she'll come appraise the collection."

"Then we get her to give us access to her collection?"

Kamal nodded. "Whatever it takes."

• • • •

"Hello, Sophia Hadad speaking. Who's calling?"

Nicolette smiled. "Bonjour. My name is Madam Nayla. I was referred to you, as I am in need of an art appraiser."

"Ah, I see," Sophia replied. "How may I help you?"

"My husband passed away recently," Nicolette began. "He left behind a collection of paintings, and I would like to know their worth."

"Certainly. I can help you with that. My schedule is often full, but I can spare you a few minutes to check the collection."

"Tomorrow morning?" Nicolette asked. "Is that possible? Eight o'clock?"

There was a rustling of papers. "Actually? Yes, I can stop by tomorrow morning before my appointments of the day. Just give me your location, and I'll meet you there."

Nicolette rattled off the street address, thanked her, and hung up the phone.

"Excellent," Kamal said. "We're not going to be here when she shows up tomorrow."

Nicolette raised an eyebrow. "Just leave her hanging?"

Kamal smiled. "You don't catch a fish on the first cast. We're going to pique her interest before we set the hook."

• • • •

"May I speak to the lady of the house?"

"I'm sorry, but Lady Nayla cannot come to the phone."

"Unbelievable!" Sophia's anger bubbled to the surface as her voice rose in intensity. "I showed up for the appointment she set, and the gate was locked!"

"I'm sorry," Kamal said softly. "Lady Nayla is still recovering."

"I don't care! I will not stand for this kind of disrespect! My time is valuable, and . . . "

"I apologize that Madam could not meet with you. Would it be possible to reschedule?"

"Absolutely not!" Sophia's scowl came through the phone. "Never in my entire life or career has someone shown such disregard for my time!"

"I understand, but again, I'm sorry . . . "

Click.

Kamal was greeted with a dial tone as the phone went dead. He put the receiver back on the base.

"She hung up on you?"

"Yes, but I expected that." Kamal looked up at Nicolette. "Let's wait a few hours, and call her back. Are you ready to turn up the heat?"

"Absolutely."

• • • •

"Hello, Miss Hadad?"

"Speaking."

"This is Mrs. Nayla. I'm sorry I wasn't able to meet with you this morning, but . . . "

"You!" Sophia's instantly changed. "You have some nerve calling me back after what you did!"

"I know, and I apologize, but there was an emergency, and I had to go to the hospital."

"Some excuse!" Sophia lowered her voice a bit, but her voice was still grating. "Unless they're on death's bed, I expect people to keep their appointments as a professional courtesy. My time is very valuable!"

"I understand," Nicolette said. "Would it be possible to reschedule for tomorrow morning?"

There was a moment of silence. "Absolutely not."

"Can you not understand that I was physically unable to be there?" Nicolette faked a quiet sob. "How could someone with your reputation be so heartless and cold?"

Sophia paused.

"I didn't mean to disappoint you, but I do need your services. Please," Nicolette said.

"I will be there at eight. And I expect someone to meet me there."

• • • •

The next morning, Kamal stood in the doorway, looking at Sophia Hadad, the professional art appraiser. Once again, she looked ready for business. A pair of glasses perched on top of her head. Standing next to Sophia was a younger man, wearing a suit, and carrying a briefcase.

"Just a minute," Kamal said. "Let me check again. Lady Nayla is still recovering."

"Recovery or not," Sophia said, "I expect people to keep their appointments!"

From the threshold, Sophia could see a swirl of color, and a pair of women's legs appeared on the stairs. Kamal looked up, glanced over at Sophia, and nodded. The mysterious figure then quickly turned and disappeared.

Kamal returned to the front door and sighed. "She says she is grateful you're here, but she cannot see you right now."

Sophia snorted. "You're wasting my time! Why did she invite me here in the first place?"

"I understand your frustration," Kamal said soothingly. "Let me at least show you the collection." He stepped aside and motioned Sophia and her companion through the door, closing it behind him.

Kamal pointed to the first alcove, where a large painting hung, high-lighted with spotlights.

"I've been told this piece is . . . "

"Yes of course," Sophia interrupted. "I'm familiar with Czachórski. I have a few of his pieces myself." She sighed. "What else is there?"

Kamal brought them around the first floor, showing each piece, as Sophia scribbled notes on a pocket notepad. Some of them caught her attention more than others. Mentally, she was making notes of which ones she might be able to buy and resell, or add to her own collection. Possibly all of them.

Above the fireplace mantle hung a large painting that pulled Sophia's eyes up from her notepad. The portrait was of a beautiful young woman wearing a short, blue velvet dress, looking forlornly out a window. The detail in it was almost photorealistic. Her loneliness seemed palpable through the brush strokes.

"Who did this? It's exquisite!" As Sophia inspected the painting, her mood began to lighten.

"That was done by a young French painter, not far from where Madam is from. His name escapes me at the moment."

"I've never heard of it. It's incredible work, though, for an unknown artist."

They continued around the mansion until they had viewed everything. When they were done, they circled back around to the foyer.

"Is this all there is?" Sophia asked, still somewhat irritated at the disappointment of not meeting her client. She betrayed no interest in the other paintings, in case it would affect their sale.

"As far as I know, yes. I will verify, however, and get back to you."

"Please do," she said flatly. "I have yet to be proven this isn't a colossal waste of time. I simply cannot work with someone who won't even meet me face to face."

"Oh no, Madam Nayla is most serious about your services. She's just . . . "

"Just what?"

"As I stated before, she's still dealing with the grief of losing her husband. I'm sure she will come around."

"I would hope so! I cannot discuss the collection with her until she does. Speaking of," Sophia said, lowering her voice, "may I ask what happened to her husband?"

"Lady Nayla's husband was a businessman in France, and I'm afraid I'm not at liberty to comment on the circumstances surrounding his death."

Sophia sighed. "Very well, mister . . . "

"I'm the groundskeeper. Call me Hassan."

"Yes, well . . . Mr. Hassan . . . please inform Mrs. Nayla I have little patience, grief or not."

"I understand. Thank you for keeping the appointment." Kamal waited until Sophia and her companion had turned and left before closing the door behind him.

"How was that?" came a voice behind him.

"Perfect. Enough to pique interest."

Nicolette nodded. "This will be entertaining."

• • • •

"Sophia Hadad speaking."

"Hello, this is Mrs. Nayla. I'm sorry I didn't see you this morning. I just wanted to call and apologize."

"I see. I'd hoped I could have talked with you in person."

"I apologize for the misunderstanding," Nicolette began. "I didn't mean to waste your time. But there are days when I cannot bear to be in the presence of other people. In fact, I am usually better off alone." There was a pause. "I do still want you to evaluate the entire collection, if you're willing."

"I'd like to ask you a question—your collection includes some rare paintings. Do you merely want them appraised, or are you interested in selling them?"

"They're not mine, they're his. Everything can go."

Sophia paused for a second. "Are you sure?"

"I don't want anything that will remind me of him. That part of my life is over. When everything is gone, I'm going to sell this house and move back to France."

"I think I can help you, then. I'm excited to be working with this collection, and getting to know more about it—and you."

Nicolette hung up the phone and smiled. "She's still considering it!"

Kamal grinned. "Time to throw another cast. If she hasn't given up by now, she's going to bite."

• • • •

The next week, they arranged another meeting with Sophia. When she arrived at the mansion, Kamal met her at the door and ushered her in.

"Is this meeting going to be more productive than the last?" Sophia sighed.

"I certainly hope so. Since your visit last week, she has had a bit of a reprise."

"Wonderful. Lead the way."

Kamal led Sophia through the foyer and into a parlor, which had wide French doors that opened onto a patio, overlooking a garden. On the patio was a table with two ornate chairs, and a full tea serving tray, all prepared and polished.

"This looks wonderful," Sophia commented. "Madam Nayla certainly has good taste."

"Please, take a seat, I will go announce your arrival."

With that, Kamal disappeared as she settled into the comfy chair. She enjoyed the bright sunshine and light breeze, taking in the smells of the small garden with delight.

But after a while, Sophia was getting tired of waiting. And after an hour, she'd had enough.

She stood, picked up her briefcase, and began walking towards the house, with the intention to leave and never come back. Anger burned her cheeks, and Sophia could feel her pride being insulted yet again.

Moments later, Kamal appeared. "I trust your meeting was more productive this time?"

"There was no meeting!" Sophia fumed. "I can't do business like this! I'm sorry, but tell Madam I'm no longer interested. I have better ways to spend my time."

"Madam might not be able to express it, but I believe she's very thankful for your help."

"I don't think you understand," Sophia said hotly. "Paintings are different from property. An art appraisal is not like a house appraisal. Art collections are very personal, very individualized, and for me to get a proper evaluation, I need to know who the collector is, what they're like, why they bought the pieces they did."

"If you knew the hardships she's gone through," Kamal said softly, "you might understand a bit better."

Sophia frowned, but took the folder from Kamal. "Is she normally this reclusive?"

Kamal ignored the question. "Is there anything else you need?"

"I'm in need of patience because mine is running out."

"I'm very sorry, but can you come back tomorrow? Please?"

Sophia's lips pursed.

"Fine," she said.

• • • •

The next morning, as Sophia pulled into the mansion's driveway, she was met by Kamal before she got out of her car.

Sophia rolled down her window. "Is there something wrong?"

"I have a personal family emergency to attend to. I'm willing to give you the keys to the mansion to do your work."

"Can't Madam Nayla meet me at the door?"

Kamal shook his head. "No, she'd rather not be disturbed. Here," he handed Sophia a keychain with half a dozen keys on it. "If it were not an emergency, I wouldn't ask you to do this, but Madam trusts you."

"Should I announce my arrival?"

"That won't be necessary. Just make yourself at home. Here's my phone number if you need anything." Kamal produced a folded piece of paper with numbers scribbled on it, and handed it over. Then he turned and began walking.

"Wait!" Sophia called. "What do I do?"

Without turning around, Kamal waved. "Just do what you need to." Then he was gone.

Sophia parked her car and slowly approached the front of the house. Sure enough, when she'd gotten to the front door, it was locked. She cautiously unlocked the door with the keys she'd been given and called loudly through the door.

"Madam Nayla! It's me, Sophia Hadad, the art appraiser."

No response. She sighed and entered, closing the door behind her.

After she'd pulled a few pieces down and had begun inspecting them with a magnifying glass, there was a series of noises from one of the rooms down the hall.

Sophia gently put her tools down and stood up from the table. The silence was eerie, as she knew Madam Nayla was somewhere in the house.

Three hours later, when Sophia had finished what he needed for the day, she packed her things and made her way to the main entrance again. The house was still dead silent.

"I'm done for the day, Madam Nayla," Sophia called loudly. She waited a few moments for a reply, then frowned. "Would you like me to go?" Again, nothing but silence.

"Are you going to even acknowledge me!?"

There was no reply. At this point, Sophia wasn't even sure her mind wasn't playing tricks on her. She decided at that moment to find out.

She quietly made her way over to the stairs, and climbed them to the second floor landing. There was a doorway to what she assumed was a bedroom.

The door to the room was slightly ajar. Through the gap, she could make out a dresser with a mirror. There were slight noises coming from inside, like the sound of someone pacing, and quietly talking to themselves.

There, through the door, she could make out someone moving. As she crept closer, she could make out a woman standing in front of a mirror. The woman was wearing a tight deep blue velvet dress, trimmed in gold threads, that fell above her knees. Something about it struck Sophia as familiar.

As the woman turned, Sophia could see her face, and her heart leapt in her throat—she was gorgeous. But more than that, she realized where she recognized the face from. This was the same woman, in the same dress, as the mysterious portrait downstairs. It was Madam Nayla, in stunning reality. Every ringlet of hair, every swish and flow of her movement, was like a vivid painting brought to life. Sophia stood breathless, watching her every movement, captivated by this mystery of a woman.

She seemed unaware of Sophia's presence, to the point where she even looked relaxed and calm. After several minutes, Sophia thought she should leave her be.

Silently, Sophia turned and crept back towards the stairs. As she approached, her elbow knocked against the banister, and she dropped her keyring, which clattered down the stairs.

"Is that you, Sophia?" Nicolette called out from somewhere.

"Yes." Sophia turned back. "I was just—I was just leaving."

"Is that what you want?" Nicolette asked.

Sophia swallowed hard. "I was just trying to answer all these questions I have, and it's been so frustrating trying to talk to you." After a pause, she added, "You've placed so much trust in me, you've even given me the keys to your home. And I only wanted a chance to get to know you."

There was no answer at first. Slowly, the door opened, and Nicolette stepped out of her room. Her eyes were red from crying, but her movements were graceful, purposeful. Her hair spilled around her shoulders like so much wind-swept shadow, highlighting her perfectly shaped face.

"I know I haven't been much of a host."

"I'm glad to see you're OK," Sophia stammered. "I've, uh, worked through cataloging the collection. Some of these pieces will fetch a very nice price on the market."

"What do you think, Miss Hadad? What is the meaning of all this?"

Sophia was caught slightly off guard. "What? Haven't you ever thought about what the purpose of collecting art is?"

Nicolette drew in close to her, her smoldering gaze never wavering. "But what do you say your purpose for collecting art is?"

From that close, Sophia could smell her perfume, and almost feel her breath like an enormous weight. Her head spun. She felt disoriented and energized at the same time.

"I—I'm not sure I know what to say."

Nicolette just shook her head. "I know." She disappeared again, leaving Sophia to mull over that thought longer than she needed to.

• • • •

Over the next two weeks, Sophia worked through appraising each piece of the collection—checking the market, talking to prospective buyers. In the back of her mind, she was contemplating which of the pieces would be valuable enough to keep for herself. Over time, Sophia had begun to be more comfortable with Nicolette's random appearances around the house, but she could never really be sure what Madam was doing at any given moment.

Madam Nayla's mood seemed to change with the day. Sometimes she would be curious and attentive, and other days she was distant and mysteriously quiet. Though she tried to convince herself it was to better assess the paintings, Sophia found herself becoming more and more interested in personal affairs. The more she talked to Nicolette, the longer their conversations lasted, to the point where they sometimes stretched on into the night.

To Sophia, the woman and the art had become one. Her entire world had become consumed with these paintings, to the point where she found herself at home less and less, and at the Mansion with Nicolette more and more. When she looked at her own art collection, she somehow saw Nicolette's soul in every painting. Her face was haunting, day and night. Her voice echoed through Sophia's head. Sometimes she would even catch herself staring at a Victorian portrait of a woman who looked like Nicolette, and having imaginary conversations with her.

It was at that point that Sophia decided that "Madam Nayla" would be the ultimate piece for her collection. Despite the taboo—and the law—Sophia had to have her.

$$\bullet \ \bullet \ \bullet \ \bullet$$

The next morning, Sophia made her way to the mansion with excitement. When she got there, it was quiet, as usual. She climbed the stairs, reaching the main entrance in seconds.

The front door, strangely, was slightly open. Sophia pushed the door aside and entered.

"Is anyone here?"

"Yes, I'll be right down," came Nicolette's voice from upstairs.

Sophia's heart was already racing, but nothing prepared her for the sight of Nicolette slowly walking down the stairs. Her face was glowing, her hair flowed and bounced like magic. She was a masterpiece come to life.

"You look amazing!" Sophia exclaimed.

Nicolette smiled. "Thank you."

Sophia's face burned red, but luckily, she remembered why she'd come. "I have something to ask you. Something very important."

Nicolette smiled and nodded. "What is it?"

"I've been thinking about this life, and about how much I've enjoyed being here, working with you. About all the things we've talked about, the appreciation for beauty we share."

"Yes?"

"When I took this assignment, my original intent was to buy your entire collection at a discount, and sell whatever I didn't want to keep for myself."

Nicolette looked surprised. "But why didn't you?"

"It would be easier to show you. . ." Sophia sighed. "Will you come outside with me? I want to take you outside this house."

Nicolette visibly recoiled. "Everything in the outside world is fake! All the fake people, fake friends . . . I just can't stand the thought of it." She dropped her gaze. "I'd rather be here, alone with you, than out there."

"No, no! I don't mean just going outside." Sophia reached out her hand. "I want to bring you someplace special. Somewhere that no one else gets to see."

"I'm not sure I understand."

"I want to show you my collection—my personal garden of beauty and serenity. There's something special about it that you must see. Then you will understand."

Nicolette thought for a second. "If you say so, I will. Nobody else really understands me like you do."

Sophia beamed. "I'll be here to pick you up at midnight."

· · · ·

At 12:00 on the dot, Sophia knocked on the door at the manor. After a few seconds, the door swung open, and Nicolette stood there to greet her, wearing a fitted lace top and skirt with high heels. Her hair swept over one of her bare shoulders, and her eyes shone like fire.

"Are you ready?"

Nicolette nodded.

She took Nicolette's hand and led her to the car, closing the door behind her. Sophia got in the driver's seat and minutes later, they pulled up to a handsome, but small, gated villa. Sophia punched a code into the gate keypad, and the gate rattled open, closing behind after they passed.

They stopped in front of the house's steps, and Sophia went around to open the car door for Nicolette. She motioned wide.

"I know it's not as nice as your mansion," Sophia said, "but there are beautiful secrets here you cannot see anywhere."

They went through the front door, into the main living area, which was nicely furnished with leather chairs, antique lamps, and a bookshelf stretching the width of the far wall. It was plain yet rustic.

"Over here," Sophia said, pointing to a sunken doorway, "is my secret garden."

Sophia stood before the bookshelf. She reached into a drawer built into the shelf. Nicolette stepped into her blind spot to peer into the draw. There was a keypad mounted into the drawer. Nicolette watched closely.

After four beeps, there was a clicking sound. Then gears whirred. And the entire bookshelf slid away to the side, revealing an iron door.

"This is my life's work," Sophia said. "My passion. My everything. In here." She turned to face another keypad. Nicolette watched each number Sophia pressed.

The door unlatched and opened. Nicolette followed Sophia.

The room within was large but not enormous. It was obviously built as an addition to the house, but Nicolette hadn't noticed it from the outside.

Every wall was covered in paintings. Rare, beautiful, and some of them she even recognized from art books. Every single painting was of some sort of beautiful woman. There was one in particular, though, that was displayed more prominently than all the others. It was the one painting they were trying to get. Nicolette recognized that it was, by itself, an amazing piece of renaissance art. But in this collection of beauty, it was the crown jewel. She understood why Sophia wouldn't part with it.

In the middle of the room was a thickly padded swivel chair, also upholstered in brown leather.

Sophia poured two drinks from a small wooden cabinet in the corner. She picked up a remote and pressed a button. Speakers in the corners of the room Nicolette hadn't noticed before brought soft, instrumental music into the atmosphere.

"Do you see this chair?" Sophia handed Nicolette her beverage and patted the chair's worn leather. "I used to sit in this chair every day and look at my paintings. I would dream about the perfect woman. I would dream of her, with all these incredible works as my muse. For years, I searched for someone. Nothing men could offer satisfied me."

"What are you saying?" Nicolette's face flushed, but she moved a bit closer. "You know that's not allowed."

Slowly, Sophia turned and looked Nicolette in the eyes. "I think I've finally found the missing piece in my life. She's standing before me now."

Nicolette reached out and placed her hands on Sophia's arms. With light caresses, she traced her fingers upwards, until her hands were resting on Sophia's shoulders.

"I've come to see you as a confidant," Nicolette said softly. "I've learned to trust you."

Sophia's heart quickened. "But what do you feel?"

"I was abused—beaten—for years by my husband." Nicolette closed her eyes. "I've never felt safe, or loved by anyone."

Keeping eye contact, she drew Sophia closer until there was no space between them. The tension was electric.

After a long moment, Sophia gave in and pressed her lips into Nicolette's. Every nerve in her body was on fire, and her heart was accelerating out of control. Her hands slid around Nicolette's waist and caressed her curves.

"Wait. Not yet." Nicolette pulled away.

Sophia's hands lingered, but she eventually let go and stepped back. "I—I'm sorry."

"No," Nicolette replied "I trust you. But this is all new to me."

"Will you stay here with me?" Sophia shook her head to clear it, her hands still trembling. "You can stay in my guest suite, and no one will bother you." She looked intently into Nicolette's eyes. "Well?"

Nicolette smiled. "Absolutely."

"I promise . . . I can make you happy here."

"I know."

After a moment of thought, Sophia snapped back to attention. "I'm sorry. I want you to know," Sophia began, "that I don't take things like relationships lightly."

"I understand," Nicolette replied. "If word got out . . ."

Sophia nodded. "Exactly. I have spent my entire life spotting forgeries. Fakes. Some of them were quite good. But they weren't the real thing. I know genuine when I see it."

"But how do you know?"

Sophia shook her head. "Experience. Sometimes it's just a gut feeling." She placed her hand on Nicolette's arm. "I have to leave on a trip to go to England for a few days, to meet a collector who's interested in buying some of your collection. But when I return, I would love to see you. Spend more time with you. Be with you."

"I will be waiting for you."

· · · ·

Sophia hurried out the sliding doors to a line of waiting taxis. The drive home was painfully slow, but eventually they got there. When she stepped out of the airport taxi onto the street in front of her home, nothing was on her mind besides seeing Nayla's face again.

She unlocked the deadbolt and opened the front door, and stepping into the hall, placed her briefcase and coat next to the door. The house was dark, so Sophia walked into the living room and flipped the lights on.

As her eyes adjusted to the light, the blood drained from her face, and her heart stopped cold.

Everything looked as he had left it, except for one thing.

The vault door was wide open.

All the art was gone. Everything. Nothing else seemed to be touched. But all of Sophia's prized collection was simply gone—empty expanses of wall were all that was left to show that anything was ever there.

Her heart pounded in her ears, until Sophia finally stumbled over to the padded chair and collapsed. In shock, she just stared at the empty walls until she finally started to realize what had happened.

Frantically, she bolted out the door and jumped into her car. Speeding off into the evening, she finally arrived at the mansion where this had all started. Every light was dark, and the gate was unlocked.

She walked up the broad staircase to the front door, but it wouldn't budge. She pulled out her keychain, and realized the keys they had given her had been removed at some point without her noticing.

Her hands trembling, Sophia looked around for a way inside, and finally spotted a window that was accessible.

She climbed to it over the hedge, and giving it a fierce yank, it opened enough to get some leverage, and pull it all the way up.

After crawling inside, the first thing she noticed was that the mansion was completely empty. All the furniture and decorations were gone. The rugs, the lamps, chairs, vases . . . everything.

Her brain still reeling, she walked through the house she had spent so many days in, until she finally stopped in front of the fireplace.

There still hanging above it, completely alone, was the painting of Nicolette wearing a blue dress.

Sophia's jaw dropped in disbelief. Everything in her world had just been violently ripped from her hands, and the only thing left was a painting of the one who had done it.

She looked more closely, her senses reeling, and saw there was a white envelope on the mantle under the painting.

She leaned forward and took the envelope in her shaking hands. Ripping it open, she pulled out a neatly folded piece of stationary with writing on it.

You thought you could never be fooled,
But were blinded by your own desires.
Your foolish pride was your destruction.
— *Nayla*

• • • •

Sophia sighed and slid deeper into the huge bathtub. Her face was streaked with tears. The only thing she wanted now was for the pain to go away.

As she read the letter one more time, her hands began to shake and go numb. Blood ran freely down her arms from the fresh cuts on her wrists, turning the bath water into a swirling red cloud. She could feel the color draining from her face as her head swam.

When she could no longer hold the letter, Sophia let it go and embraced the growing chill. Her head hung limply, and as everything slid into darkness, she took one last breath and cursed the world that had taken everything away from her. Silently, she slid into the red watery oblivion.

CHAPTER 7

SHOCK

Kamal walked into the shop and looked around. He had found a small art dealer in Paris who was willing to buy collections of paintings in bulk for a discounted price, and then split them off to resell individually for profit. Many less experienced dealers worked this way, as it allowed them access to plenty of art pieces, without having to be an expert on any one style.

Three days prior, Nicolette had filed a police report in France and told them their hotel was robbed. She told them the thieves took cash, a few personal effects, and a folder with their paintings' certificates of authenticity.

"Hello m'sieur, how may I help you?" A short, balding man stepped up to the counter, and looked Kamal up and down.

"I recently inherited a collection from my father, and I'm interested in selling off the whole lot."

The man's eyebrows worked up and down as he thought. "You want to sell an entire collection? How much?"

"I have twelve pieces, all worth a good bit on their own. I just don't want to be bothered with selling them off one-by-one."

"Anything you want to keep? Something special?"

"No," Kamal sighed. "I'm not interested in collecting. I know what they're worth, but I'm not interested in the art scene. I'd much rather travel."

"Ah, I see." The man wiped his forehead with a handkerchief. "I don't blame you, really. Do you have photos of anything in the collection?"

"Yes, I've got them right here." Kamal gave the man a folder of papers with photographs. "I've had most of them appraised. All the paperwork there."

"You know," said the man after looking through the folder, "I'm going to need to have them authenticated. I recognize some of these artists already though. I should have no problems finding buyers for them."

"I understand. I've already had them authenticated by an appraiser."

"You have all the certificates?"

"I do," Kamal said. "Everything's there. I just need someone to take them off my hands."

"Well," the shopkeeper said, "I might be able to help you, then. My name's Francois. I've been selling and buying art for twenty one years, and my reputation is second to none. My customers expect no less."

"Of course. I would assume you know what you're doing."

Francois puffed his chest up, which looked comical with his short stature. "I will do my best to make the transaction easy for you. I give you my word." He stuck his hand out eagerly.

"I'm sure you will," Kamal replied, shaking the man's hand. "I'll be in touch, but you can expect me to bring them by the end of the month." He shook his head. "It's taking some time to get everything moved. You know how that goes."

Francois nodded. "Yes, of course. Here," he added, handing Kamal a business card, "let me know when you're settled, and we can work out the details."

"Fantastic. Thanks for your help."

As Kamal left, the shopkeeper let out a low whistle.

"What was that about?" A young man, about twenty, stuck his head through the door behind the counter.

"None of your business," Francois snapped. "We just might have run into some good luck."

"I don't know. I don't trust that guy."

"Joseph, what do you know? Just because you're my son doesn't mean you can read people. I've been doing this—"

"Yeah, I know." Joseph frowned. "I still don't like the guy."

"You like money though."

Joseph just shook his head and walked back to the rear of the shop.

• • • •

"These look incredible!" Nicolette lifted up a painting and pointed to it. "They copied everything exactly, even down to the paint on the edges and the tacking on the canvas!"

"Of course." Kamal nodded. "They're the best in the business. If you want a copy to just hang on your wall, those are easy to find. If you want to fool an appraiser, you have to have the best."

"Did you find a buyer for them?"

"Yes, in Paris. After you filed the police report saying the certificates were stolen, I knew it wouldn't be difficult to find one. We can use the certificates from the real paintings to sell these for ten times what we paid to have them made."

"Wait. You want to use the certificates from the real paintings to sell the fake ones?"

"Basically, yes. The shop has no way of knowing the paintings are fake if the certificates are real."

"Ingenious!" Nicolette flashed a bright smile. "So what are we going to do with the real paintings?"

"First, I have to bring that special one to Al-Fahad, and get paid for that."

"Right," Nicolette said. "But then how are we going to sell the originals without certificates of authenticity?"

"We'll report the fake painting sales, let the police get the certificates back, and then use them again to sell the originals. Double the profit!"

"No words!"

Kamal smiled.

• • • •

"We have the painting you requested," Kamal said. "We handed it off to your men in the back. Everything's been taken care of."

Al-Fahad chuckled. "I knew you could do it. You always do. Of course, I never doubted you for a moment." He tapped Kamal on the shoulder and motioned towards the side of the casino.

They sat at a table in a darkened booth, where they could easily see people enter, but couldn't be seen themselves from the entrance.

"So everything went smoothly?" Al-Fahad asked. "There's no damage?"

Kamal nodded. "Everything went perfectly, and no, there was no damage. We took everything she had in her collection, and brought the one you wanted, as requested."

"Perfect. Here is your reward, my young friend." Al-Fahad handed another leather briefcase to Kamal.

Kamal nodded. "Life is what you take from it."

"I couldn't agree more," Al-Fahad replied. "And as for our appraiser friend who refused to sell the painting? Miss Hadad?"

"Her ego could not bear her fate. She was too weak for this world, so she put herself out of her misery." Kamal said. "She slit her wrists because she couldn't live with her mistakes."

"Is that so?" Al-Fahad shook his head. "I wasn't expecting that. Regardless, you've done another excellent job." Al-Fahad stood, and as he did so, Kamal stood as well. "As usual, I will be in contact when I need you again."

"I appreciate it. Be sure to give your buyer my regards." Kamal shook Al-Fahad's hand, and left the casino, briefcase close at hand.

• • • •

"Leave me alone! Let me go!"

A pair of policemen held Francois by the arms, who was struggling with all his might, to no avail.

"You're under arrest for fraud and theft," the bigger policeman boomed.

"That's impossible! I've never cheated anyone in my life!"

"You've been reported for fencing forged and stolen paintings and—"

"Forged paintings? I have signed certificates of authenticity for every piece of art I sell!"

"You'll have your day in court." The policeman slapped handcuffs on Francois and gave him a shove, sending him thudding into the wall.

The commotion continued until they finally forced Francois out the door and stuffed him into the back of a police car. Outside the shop, a small crowd had amassed to see what was going on. Some were shouting at the police, some were jeering at Francois.

Standing there, talking to a policeman on the sidewalk, was Nicolette.

Joseph, the shopkeeper's son, watched her converse with the policeman. His vision turned red, and his heart pounded fiercely. His hands clenched into fists, but there was nothing he could do while the policemen were still there. He slipped away from the crowd, back around to the side of the shop.

"We're sorry this happened, madame," said the officer. "We've got the culprit in custody, and we'll contact you when we know more. At least you still have your original paintings, so no harm there."

"Thank you so much," gushed Nicolette. "I'm just glad he was caught!"

The policeman tipped his hat, and began walking away. Nicolette looked across the crowd and nodded. There, in the throng of people, was Kamal.

Kamal wove through the people who had gathered and approached Nicolette. "They should give us back the certificates once the case clears, and we can finish selling them like we intended."

Nicolette nodded. "It might take a few weeks, but we'll get everything back eventually, right?"

"Yes," Kamal answered. "There's nothing more we can do here. Let's get some drinks.and Relax."

• • • •

The rooftop bar was lined with huge windows overlooking the night skyline. Young people were milling about, talking over the music and having a good time.

"Cheers!" Kamal lifted his glass high, and smiled. "We did it."

Nicolette followed suit. "Here's to the good life," Nicolette said. "I still can't believe we pulled that off."

Kamal looked out over the city skyline from the rooftop cafe, and shook his head. "Did you really think we couldn't?"

She leaned back and laughed. "I don't think that ever crossed my mind!" Taking a sip, she sighed contentedly. "But I do wonder what happened to the art dealer we screwed over."

Kamal's mood darkened a little. "I wouldn't worry about it. They'll figure it out eventually."

Nicolette nodded. "I'm sure they will." She placed her glass down and stood up, showing off her generous curves in a low-cut, skin-tight white dress. "Come on, Kamal, let's dance."

At first, he just shook his head. "You know I don't dance." But the more Nicolette began to move with the music, the more he didn't want her to dance by herself.

Kamal took a quick look around and joined her. Nicolette's gyrations rose in intensity with the music, drawing the attention of most of the young men. Kamal pretended not to notice.

As the song ended, Nicolette pulled Kamal close, wrapping her arms around his neck with a giggle. "Come on! Quit acting like that! Aren't you happy?"

With their eyes locked, they could almost see each other's souls. Each broken in their own way. Kamal thought about how hard life had been to both of them. Somehow, they had managed to turn all that pain into success together. Kamal knew he would always be there for her, and she for him- even if it meant death. The look in her eyes told the same story, but it was something they would never get to speak out loud.

Kamal flashed a smile. "I'm glad you're here with me. I couldn't have done it without you." He paused for a second, still looking into her eyes. "You're amazing."

Nicolette spun around and made her way back to the table, shooting him a glance over her shoulder. "I know."

CHAPTER 7 - SHOCK

When they had finished their drinks, Kamal threw the bartender a tip, and directed Nicolette to the door. The rooftop pub was serviced by a large glass elevator that slid its way down the side of the building, letting them enjoy the view all the way down.

When they reached the ground floor, they made their way through the hotel's lobby out into the street, where traffic flowed back and forth. Kamal motioned to the left. "This way, we parked over here."

The air was balmy as they rounded the corner and walked to where their car was parked, but before they could make the length of the block, someone stepped from the shadows.

"Excuse me," Kamal said, sidestepping him.

"You ruined my father's life!" Joseph pulled his hoodie back. "It's only fair you lose yours!"

Joseph whipped out a switchblade knife, lunged towards Nicolette, and twisted the blade into her stomach.

Nicolette froze. Her mouth hung open in shock. For a long moment, everything stopped, and Joseph's eyes locked with hers, his face contorted with rage.

Then just as quickly, Joseph yanked the knife away, turned, and flung it as hard as he could.

"NOOO!!!" Kamal rushed to Nicolette's side. Blood ran from the wound, and as Kamal applied pressure, her fitted white dress quickly began turning bright red as her life flowed from the wound.

"I hope you rot in hell!" screamed Joseph, as he took off running.

Nicolette's eyes rolled back in her head. She strained a breath and coughed. She moved her mouth but no words came.

In an instant, Kamal's entire world started to come apart. Scenes of the orphanage flashed in his mind. He remembered Nicolette, remembered the rage he felt when she was raped. "No! God, please, no! No . . God, please . . ." For a split second, Kamal wanted to chase down the attacker and make him pay. In fact, he wanted to squeeze the life out of every man that had hurt the woman he loved. He wanted to burn the world down, and Kamal didn't care if it took him with it. His heart pounded, his fists clenched, and for a split second, Kamal was torn. But vengeance wouldn't save her

He managed to pick her up, blood still going everywhere, and carry her the last few feet to the car. Somehow he got her in the passenger's seat, but everything was covered in blood and hard to get a grip on.

"Stay with me, Nicol, I'm going to get you help."

For the first time since his childhood, tears flowed down Kamal's face. Losing Nicolette would mean losing the only thing in his life that mattered. The fear of living without her was a kind of fear he had never felt before. His bloodied hands fumbled for his keys. Kamal slammed the car into gear, and with a squelch of tires, blasted into the city.

CHAPTER 8

DESPERATE

Kamal looked out the large window across the cityscape. Paris was beautiful as always, but he could not enjoy it. Kamal turned and looked at the machines next to the hospital bed. They were contentedly beeping in rhythm. In the bed, buried under blankets, was Nicolette.

Just yesterday, they were celebrating. The entire art scandal—fooling Sophia Hadad, stealing the masterpiece, reselling the forgeries—had resulted in a huge payoff. Months of work, research, traveling, and working on keeping the charade going, almost completely undone by a loose end that Kamal hadn't tied up.

Kamal played the scene over and over in his mind. They had just finished getting the art dealer in France arrested for selling their forgeries. He remembered arriving at the hotel, the rooftop party, the dancing, the ride down the elevator.

Kamal especially remembered the loose end he hadn't accounted for—Joseph, the art dealer's son. He remembered the look on his face, the glint of steel in the moonlight, the look on Nicolette's face as the knife sunk into her abdomen. Kamal remembered the horrific dash to the hospital, and blood everywhere. Every detail of last night was burned into Kamal's brain.

"I'm sorry that I let this happen," Kamal said quietly. "This is all my fault." The only answer was Nicolette's soft breathing.

Kamal pounded his fist into his palm. "I should have been more careful. I don't make mistakes . . . Should not have happened. Cannot let it happen again . . . I cannot make mistakes!"

A noise in the hallway snapped Kamal out of his thoughts. Seconds later, a doctor appeared.

"She's doing OK," the doctor said calmly. "We managed to stop the internal bleeding. The injury left a lot of damage, but we've managed to stabilize her. It's just going to take some time for her to heal. "

"Thank you." Kamal looked back at Nicolette's face and shook his head. "I just . . ."

"She's going to be OK. She's resting. The best thing you can do is be strong for her when she wakes up."

Kamal nodded. *I'll always be here for her.*

The doctor nodded and left the room, leaving Kamal alone with Nicolette.

Sitting on the bed, Kamal looked at Nicolette's pallid face, and a burning fire began to rise in him again. "This mistake would have cost me my life. Because you are my one reason to live." He shook his head and stood up. "This will never happen again. I swear to you."

Kamal was startled out of his thoughts by the telephone ringing. Cautiously, he picked it up.

"Hello?"

"Kamal!" He recognized Al-Fahad's voice on the other end. "I heard what happened. Is she okay?"

Kamal sighed. "She will be."

"I'm glad to hear that. But I'm sure you're wondering why I called."

"I know you, Al-Fahad. I'm sure there's a reason."

"I have a very special, very difficult job for you. Do you think you're up for it? Especially after . . ."

"Yes. Of course I am," Kamal said. "What happened changes nothing."

"I see. But if you're caught," Al-Fahad said, "we cannot rescue you." There was a heavy pause over the receiver. "The government will sentence you to life in prison."

Kamal thought hard. The stakes were rising. But with enough planning, he could do anything. He glanced over to where Nicolette was sleeping. Something stirred deep within. This was a chance to right this wrong. This was his chance to prove how intelligent, how capable, and how superior he was to all other men.

Kamal took a deep breath. "What do I need to do?"

"We want you to transport some crates. Our contact in Turkey is having difficulty smuggling product from the Netherlands through Turkey into Lebanon. Understandably, going through Syria isn't an option. I'd like you to get the shipments from Turkey to Beirut port."

"'Product,'" Kamal chuckled. "Is that what I think it is?"

"It doesn't matter what it is," Al-Fahad replied. "Just don't get caught. You'll be paid well. Can I count on you? Are you in?"

"Yeah, I'm in. How many crates are there, and where do I pick them up?"

"I will have my personal assistant, Adonis, contact you and work with you. He'll fill you in on everything you need to know. I'm sure you will find a way to accomplish this without getting caught. Oh, and Kamal?"

"Yes?"

"Don't get caught."

• • • •

Two days later, Kamal arrived back in Lebanon while Nicolette was still recovering in the hospital. After looking through maps and charts and figuring out where the border guards would be watching, he had formulated a plan.

The first part was to find the right boat. But as he stood on the dock seeing it in person, Kamal wasn't too sure about it. He looked at the crusty fishing boat and shook his head. "I don't believe I trust this heap."

"Of course it's good! This has a solid motor. Do you like it?"

The boat was large enough, and it did have a big enough engine to make it through rough waters. Kamal didn't really want a boat that looked new either, as that would draw attention. But he wasn't going to tell the old man that. Kamal had done his research and knew the company was on the verge of bankruptcy. Still, the company was well-known and had survived twenty years in the business. But higher competition with lower prices had eaten away their business. And now it showed.

"OK, I guess this will do."

"Excellent!" The grubby old fisherman flashed a smile, showing several missing teeth. "You won't regret it!"

Kamal handed him a check—from a fake company with a fake name—and the deal was done. Kamal was now the owner of a fishing company. The next step was going to be figuring out how to run the boat up along the coast without being stopped.

"Can your crewmen be trusted?"

"Sure!" the old man wheezed. "They're hard workers. Strong backs."

"Thanks," Kamal said. "Anyone to look out for?"

"Have to watch the young guys . . . they like to blow their money on women and booze."

Kamal smiled. "Understood."

For the next few days, Kamal spent his time becoming familiar with operating the fishing boat and talking with the deckhands. None of them looked reliable, but as long as they didn't cause trouble, Kamal was happy. They kept working, and Kamal watched everything they did.

At the end of the week, Kamal assembled the fishermen in the ramshackle office by the dock.

"Tomorrow, we're taking a detour. I just want you to keep working like you normally do." He looked around at the six men in front of him. "The only thing we're doing differently is we're going to pick up a shipment in Turkey first thing in the morning. Then we'll head south and do a run like we normally would."

"Why should we?" piped up one of the deckhands. "If we get caught up that way, they're gonna want to know why. That's bad news. We don't need any trouble!"

"I'm willing to give the crew half of my cut, if you can do it and not ask questions." He looked around again, making sure to make eye contact with each man. "I'm talking half a million dollars here. And if we get stopped," he continued, "I'll take the blame for it."

There were a few seconds of silence as the men looked back and forth amongst themselves.

"I won't be upset if you don't want to do it," Kamal said with a slow nod. "Just walk out now, and nothing more needs to be said. There's no dishonor in that."

More silence, and some of the men shifted uncomfortably in their seats, but no one made a move.

"Right then. As far as you're concerned, you see nothing, you know nothing. Be here at 5:00 a.m."

• • • •

"You want us to do *what?*"

Kamal smiled. "I want to hire divers to recover something that was lost off of a boat. But I need it done at a certain time, so that the authorities will not bother us."

The man looked at Kamal and frowned. "I'm not sure about this."

"Whatever your normal hourly rate is, I'll quadruple it. I'll even pay you half up front."

The man raised an eyebrow. "Go on."

"If the cargo isn't recovered, or gets confiscated by the port authorities, you will be responsible for it. So I need your absolute best men."

"Assuming we agree to do this," the man said, "what would we have to do?"

"I'll charter a boat to get you to the location, I'll arrange for delivery and pickup, and I'll pay you in cash." Kamal's smile faded. "It's about forty minutes from Beirut, not too far offshore. I'll have a marker there for your men to find it, and the boat captain will bring you to it." He leaned in closer. "I just need someone who can recover the cargo without incident, and without questions."

The man thought for a second, then nodded. "Okay. I have just the men for the job."

• • • •

"I don't think they're going to let us pass." Concern shot across the face of one of the boat's crew members as he peered into the distance.

Thinking about the shipment of crates they had picked up in Turkey an hour before, Kamal looked at the deckhand and nodded. "You made sure to bury those crates under all the fish, right?"

"Yes . . ."

"Okay then, I'll handle it. Just stay out of the way."

A few minutes later, the fishing boat chugged and sputtered as the motor stopped. A Turkish police boat slid up alongside them, and a couple of stern looking officers came to the side. One of them held up a small bullhorn.

"*Nereye gidiyorsun?* Where are you going?"

"We're just trying to get back home!" Kamal yelled back.

"Why are you so far north?"

"We can't go back until we have a full load, or they'll fire us!"

"Do you have anything on board?"

Kamal looked around, then laughed. "We have fish!"

The two officers conversed briefly, then turned back to them.

"We'd like to inspect your boat. Prepare to be boarded."

One of the officers, holding a rope, jumped over to Kamal's boat and quickly tied it off. He approached Kamal. "We've watched you for a while. We know you're carrying something."

"Feel free to look for yourselves," Kamal said, motioning to the storage hold hatch in the deck.

The officer snorted, then with a grunt, yanked the hatch open. He recoiled instantly when the only thing that greeted him was the overwhelming smell of fish.

"Would you like one to bring home to the wife?" Kamal said. "They're freshly caught!"

The officer scowled, then motioned to the other officer. "Check below." He continued to glare at Kamal. "Let me see your papers."

"Absolutely." Kamal ducked into the boat's wheelhouse and returned with a plastic bag containing his business license, boat registration, and a fake passport. He handed them to the officer, who sorted through them and handed them back.

"Everything in order?" Kamal said smoothly, but received no answer.

A few minutes later, the second officer emerged from below deck empty-handed. The first officer, visibly irritated, turned to Kamal and stuck a finger in his chest. "We know who you are now, we'll be keeping an eye on you."

"OK." Kamal smiled awkwardly. "Good."

The officer scowled but said nothing. Then with a signal to the police boat, the officers untied the rope and hopped back across. Kamal waved as they pulled away.

When they were finally out of sight, the big deckhand came and approached Kamal. "They didn't find anything?"

"Don't worry, Adonis, they're just doing their jobs," Kamal replied. "They would have had to dig through a hundred kilos of fish before they found anything."

Adonis flashed a half-smile. "Heh. That would have been worth it to see."

"Almost," Kamal chuckled. "We're going to pull into Beirut in about an hour and a half. Do you remember what I told you to do when we got there? You know they're going to inspect the boat."

"Yeah, sure. I'll take care of it."

"Perfect." Kamal slapped Adonis on the shoulder. "I know I can count on you. But before that . . ."

Kamal motioned to Adonis, and they walked back into the boat's wheelhouse. Kamal pointed to a gray box with a screen on it mounted to the dash. "How close are we to the drop point?"

"This satellite location device tells us exactly where we are by latitude and longitude. When we get to this location," Adonis continued, pointing to a notepad with numbers scribbled on it, "we'll be somewhere off the coast between Tripoli and Beirut. That's where we'll make the drop."

"That's a nice piece of equipment," Kamal said with a nod. "Where'd you find that?"

"We picked it up from an American dealer. Brand new technology." Adonis looked at the screen, then back to Kamal. "We should be there in about an hour."

"Excellent. We should have all the containers uncovered and ready to go by then. We can make the drop and pull into the harbor." Kamal looked back towards the hold. "And you're sure the divers will find them before something happens? We picked that spot specifically to make it easy for them to retrieve without being spotted. It's only about 10 or 12 meters deep."

"As long as we drop them in the right place," Adonis said, patting the GPS receiver, "they'll find it."

• • • •

"Here it is!" yelled Adonis over the clatter of the boat's engine. "We're right on top of it!"

Kamal cut the engine, and the boat rumbled to a stop. "OK," he shouted. "Let's go!"

In seconds, they had the gantry crane unsecured and unwinding cable. Kamal dropped down below deck and grabbed a length of rope. Next to the well pumps was a stack of crates, much like the fish crates, but labeled in Dutch text. Kamal hooked the crane to one with some straps, went back above, and hoisted it across onto the deck. As soon as it touched town, one of the crew was there unstrapping it. They popped the lid off and pulled a large waterproof vinyl sack out, while another man tied fist-sized fishing net weights made of lead onto the bag. Once it had been weighted, the two crew hoisted it up to the rail and tossed the bag over.

After twenty-five minutes and ten sacks, they were done. Adonis secured the crane while Kamal shouted orders to the men.

"What are you looking at? Let's go! Start prepping crates for the fish! We'll be in port in less than an hour! And make sure you burn those Dutch crates! We don't want anyone finding them." The crew bustled about, doing their normal jobs lining up crates and lids, and prepping the boat for docking.

Kamal turned back to the steering wheel and picked up a handheld radio mic. "Fish are in the water," he said, clicking the mic's thumb button.

"Acknowledged, we're on our way," came a static reply. Adonis looked at him and nodded. "The divers should get here before we reach Beirut."

Forty-five minutes later, the boat slid up to the dock, and Kamal motioned to two deck hands to tie it off. To the right of the dock was a stretch of wharf fronted with a handful of squat office buildings. To the left was a ramshackle warehouse, surrounded by broken old crates and debris.

The dock they were delivering to in Beirut was old and run-down, but still did plenty of business. The big warehouses were mixed in with ancient fishing shacks and yards full of shipping containers. It was like a maze, but Kamal had been observant, and knew who every building belonged to.

As they prepared to unload, Kamal could hear voices carrying across the water from not that far away. It was probably just regular dock workers on the late shift, but Kamal couldn't be sure they didn't have security. Dock police would be patrolling there as well, though he knew their shifts weren't that frequent.

Kamal swung the gantry crane over the hold and winched the basket down into the hatch. They began filling the basket with fish and dumping them into crates on the deck for shipment. When each crate was almost full, they hoisted it onto the dock. The crew on the dock then unhooked the crate, dumped buckets of ice on top of the fish, nailed the crate lid on, and lifted it into the delivery box truck.

Moments later, there was a loud commotion and shouting nearby. A police car pulled up to the dock and stopped. Four men got out and began looking around. One of them spotted Kamal and pointed toward the boat.

Without hesitation, Kamal hopped onto the pier and approached the policemen. The crew continued packing crates and carrying them over to the truck.

Kamal spoke up first. "Good evening! What seems to be the problem?"

The officer shot Kamal a glare. "It looks like all your fish are unloaded?"

"I think so, yes," Kamal replied.

"Good. Make sure you have your papers in order." He pointed, and the other policeman approached the boat. As he proceeded to search it, the first officer pulled out a clipboard and turned back to Kamal. "Where are these crates going?"

"To the market," Kamal answered. "You know, the fish market."

"OK." The officer scribbled something on the clipboard. "We need to check the truck too."

The other officers grumbled, but nodded. They walked over to where the old Volvo box truck sat, now filled with crates of fish. Kamal followed at a short distance.

"Anything besides fish in there?" The officer asked.

"It's all fish," Kamal replied. "But you know, if you want to unpack every single crate to look, you're welcome to. And by the time you finish, the fish won't be fresh any more . . . so you'd need to compensate me for losing the fish."

With a few more grumbles and gripes, the policemen eventually shook his head, turned, and left, leaving Kamal with the truck.

"Okay man," Kamal called out to the crew. "Good work. Clean the nets, stow everything on the boat, and I'll take care of the rest when I get back from the market."

With that, Kamal jumped into the box truck, fired it up, and rumbled off to pick up the cargo from the divers.

• • • •

Kamal casually straightened himself and held his hand out towards Al-Fahad, who shook it firmly.

"You've done well," Al-Fahad said with a nod. "You've always come through for me. So I need you to do another run, like the first, but with a bigger delivery." He raised an eyebrow. "You can do it, correct?"

Kamal thought about Nicolette for a moment. She was still in the hospital in Paris. He had made more than enough money on the last job to last them both for a while.

"You know it will be much riskier," Kamal replied. "Turkish police already know who I am." He looked away for a moment. "Plus, I . . . I have personal things I want to attend to."

Al-Fahad leaned back a bit, and nodded. "I understand the risks. And I also know you want to return to Paris."

Kamal looked a bit surprised, but said nothing.

"I wouldn't have asked you if I didn't think you could do it." Al-Fahad leaned in closer again. "And I wouldn't have asked if I wasn't willing to make it worth your while. So, what do you say? Can I count on you?"

Kamal took a deep breath. "Okay. I'll do it. I'll need money up front for supplies, but yes, I will do it."

"The drop off will be the same," Al-Fahad said. "We'll have another three divers recover the shipment where no one following you will see."

"That works for me," Kamal agreed.

"I don't have to remind you what will happen if you get caught."

Kamal shook his head. "No. I understand."

"Good. It will be the same pickup and dropoff locations. And since the shipment is twice the size, it will be more than twice the pay."

"Understood. Is there anything else?"

Al-Fahad paused for a moment. "I know you have some reservations. Be careful. I would hate to lose one of my best business associates."

"Don't be concerned about me," Kamal said with a wry grin. "They have to catch me first."

• • • •

"Where's Ali?" Kamal looked around the small office impatiently. "He was supposed to call me if he couldn't make it."

"I saw him three days ago," one of the deckhands chimed in.

"What was he doing?"

"Drinking and picking up girls, what else?" There was an echo of laughter in the room, but it died quickly.

"Has anyone tried calling him?" someone suggested.

"I did this morning," Kamal answered, "but he never picked up. I assumed he was on his way here."

There was a still quiet, and then Kamal continued. "Let me make a phone call first."

Kamal walked into the adjacent office, closed the door, and picked up the receiver. He punched in a number.

"Al-Fahad? This is Kamal."

"Yes, do you have news?"

"One of my crew didn't show up this morning. Ali."

"I was actually about to call you. He was arrested by the Lebanese police."

"I was warned about that," Kamal said. "Do you think he talked to them?"

"Almost certainly. Cocaine possession is capital crime. Unless he cuts a deal."

"OK then." Kamal's mind processed what that meant. "So I have to go in assuming they know my current plan, and will try to stop me."

"Precisely."

"In some ways," Kamal thought, "this might work to my advantage. If I know they're going to be looking for me, then I also know where they will be and what they're looking for."

"OK," Kamal said into the phone. "I can handle it. I'll have to hire some extra men who don't know what I'm planning. I'll take care of it."

He hung up the phone and sighed. After a long silence, Kamal nodded. "OK. Change of plans."

Walking back into the area where the men were waiting, Kamal smiled. "Adonis, you come with me. Everybody else, we're not working today. I'll see you tomorrow."

There was some grumbling, and a few curses about Ali probably being the reason. But everyone exited until only Kamal and Adonis were left.

"So things went south because of Ali?" Adonis asked.

"Yeah. We're going to formulate a new plan, and I'm going to need your help to get it done in time. And let's hope we didn't miscalculate anything."

Adonis nodded. "Just tell me what to do."

• • • •

"They're gaining on us!" Tension rose in Kamal's voice as he unconsciously urged the fishing boat to go faster. But despite it running wide open, the tired fishing boat was no match for a military cutter.

Some radio noise broke the tension. Kamal briefly looked at the police radio scanner. It was a simple piece of technology, but it had served its purpose.

Minutes dragged on with the cutter drawing closer until within shooting range. Instead, they were targeted with blinding light from the cutter's two giant spotlights.

"HALT IMMEDIATELY!" blared a deafening loudspeaker. "THIS IS THE TURKISH POLICE! STOP OR WE WILL OPEN FIRE!"

Kamal nodded and pulled back the throttle lever. The ancient diesel engine sputtered, chugged, and wheezed to an idle.

Through the slight mist, Kamal could see four or five officers with rifles pointed directly at him. As the cutter drew alongside, three of them jumped aboard and began shouting orders.

"Don't move! Keep your hands where we can see them! Police!"

Kamal and the three deckhands with him lifted their arms. One of the officers approached them, and in the glare of the deck lighting, he could see that the officer was resting his hand on a pistol at his side.

"Well, if it isn't the city boy fisherman!" The officer snarled. "How was your catch today?"

"Not bad," Kamal replied. "We were trying to get ahead of that storm before it caught us. Sorry if that's a problem."

"The only problem I have," the officer oozed, "is that I keep seeing your face in my waters. Where did you go this time?"

"Around the north shore, and then back here. We decided to cut it short because this boat couldn't handle a big storm."

"Lies!" snapped the officer. "I know where you went! One of your former employees just so happens to have a taste for women, cocaine, and fighting, and of course, he ended up in jail in Lebanon."

Kamal acted surprised. "I have no idea what you're talking about, but I know plenty of guys who will make up things to get out of a drug charge."

"We know exactly what's going on," the officer snapped. "The Lebanese police told us everything."

"If that's the case," Kamal said, "where's your proof? There's nothing but fish on this boat."

"We're going to check just to make sure," the officer sneered. "I'm not here for the contraband, although I'm sure we will find it." He pointed at Kamal. "I'm here for *you*."

"You can't arrest me." Kamal stepped back and dropped his hands. "You have no evidence!"

The officer laughed. "I'm sure we'll find something you missed. We know you picked up a shipment in Karatas."

Kamal looked uncomfortable. "What are you talking about?"

"I'm certain you weren't just getting supplies." The captain smirked. "You!" He pointed to one of the other rifle-toting men. "Search this ship inside and out! I don't care if you have to dig through every fish in it! You can do nothing. You're under arrest."

Kamal raised a hand as if to punch the captain and possibly jump overboard, but before he could even think to swing, he was staring into a rifle muzzle.

"Go ahead, try it," the captain hissed. "I'd love to see you get what's coming."

In seconds, Kamal was in handcuffs and being unceremoniously pushed aside.

The captain looked at the crewmen, who were still standing with their hands in the air. "Where do you think you're going?" he snarled.

"I'm just waiting for you to finish your search so I can go home to my wife," one of them said. "There isn't anything down there but fish."

Just then, one of the officers emerged from the lower deck hold, looking extremely disgusted.

"We found some sealed boxes with some Dutch text on them," he grunted. "God, it stinks to high heaven down there."

The captain snorted. "Are you sure?"

The officer shot him a look that would scar a lesser man. "Feel free to look for yourself," he said, dripping with sarcasm and fish slime.

"Well, how about that? Looks like we found something after all!" The captain suddenly turned to Kamal. "What's so funny?"

Kamal, fighting back a smile, shook his head. "Nothing at all."

Adonis was right, he thought. *It was totally worth it.*

"Why do you have Dutch shipping containers on your boat?"

"I found those in a junk pile somewhere," Kamal replied.

"Then you won't mind if we open them?"

The officer covered in slime disappeared again, and a few minutes later reemerged, even more unenthusiastically.

"Well?" the captain snapped.

"They're, um . . ." The officer frowned. "They're full of fish."

"They must have dropped them somewhere! Go back where they've been and search!" The captain, undeterred, grabbed Kamal and pulled him towards the police cutter. "We'll sort this out while you rot in jail!"

• • • •

"Kamal has been arrested!" The radio crackled and whizzed, then fell silent.

Adonis grabbed the handheld microphone. "Are you sure?"

"Yes," the voice replied. "We just heard from the rest of the crew—they picked him up and escorted the boat to shore."

"Roger that."

Miles away to the south, Adonis stood on the deck of a second fishing boat. He pulled the throttle back and turned to the crewman next to him. "We're about to hit the drop mark. Get the bags ready!"

In the dark, three men were dragging sacks, with weights attached, to the edge of the deck. On Adonis's signal, they heaved them, one by one, overboard.

• • • •

Kamal didn't know how long he'd been sitting in the interrogation room, but it felt like days. The tiny little box of a room had nothing in it except a table, some chairs, and a light bulb clinging to the ceiling for dear life. He hadn't been able to sleep at all, so Kamal sat and waited.

The actual interrogation had gone on for hours, but no matter what they did or asked, Kamal simply replied with "I don't know what you're talking about." After a while, they realized they weren't getting anywhere, and left him there to stew.

When the door finally opened, he was met not by two burly police officers, but by a slim, middle-aged woman.

Kamal stood and stretched. His joints didn't appreciate sitting in a metal chair for hours.

"Mr. Tamir? I'm sorry, but there must have been some kind of misunderstanding . . ."

"A misunderstanding? Is that what they're calling it?" Kamal scoffed. "They threatened me with guns! They nearly destroyed my boat."

The lady forced a smile. "I'm sure we'll take care of it, Mr. Tamir. We're very sorry. You're free to go. Follow me, please."

She turned, and Kamal followed her through the police station until they were at the front desk.

As he neared the door that separated the lobby from the desk, he caught a glimpse through a window of the police captain that had arrested him the day before. The captain appeared to be yelling at someone, and after a moment, glanced up at Kamal. The pure rage that his eyes conveyed made Kamal feel a little better about having to sit in the metal box.

"Here are your belongings," the lady said, and handed Kamal a plastic bin. He quickly flipped through his wallet, and as expected, the cash was gone. But nothing else was missing.

"Thank you," Kamal said to the lady. "Be sure to send the Captain my regards." And with that, Kamal casually strode out the door with a smile on his face.

• • • •

"I had heard you were arrested! How did you get away?" Al-Fahad leaned in with a curious look.

"Because I knew what to expect. I knew they would track me once I left Turkey, and they did. I'd registered another fishing boat under a different company name, so I had Adonis take the second boat to do the actual pickup, a day before. After he picked up, Adonis docked the boat at a different location until I got arrested. When the police began searching my boat, that was Adonis's cue to head back out to sea to drop the shipment. So when they allowed me to fly back to Lebanon, the shipment had already been delivered."

"Did they make it difficult for you while you were arrested?" Al-Fahad asked.

"They certainly weren't happy about not finding anything. I'm actually surprised they didn't plant evidence on the boat and keep me on false charges."

"Sometimes you need some luck."

• • • •

"What are you going to do with those?"

Kamal raised an eyebrow and smiled. "You know what handcuffs are for, right?"

The escort he'd picked up from his friend's house wasn't that young, but she looked cute. Cute enough. She hadn't wasted any time getting down to business. As long as she could keep Kamal from thinking about being lonely, she would do.

"Am I under arrest?" she giggled.

"That remains to be seen." Kamal stepped out of the car into the empty parking lot and breathed in the scent of the ocean.

Taking her hand, he pulled her along the path, which opened up to a quiet beach. The night air was a little cool, but the ocean waves were warm and inviting.

"I brought a blanket," Kamal said. "The atmosphere is perfect. What do you think?"

"This spot is beautiful!" Within seconds, she had removed her top and was slipping out of her skirt. Kamal spread out the blanket while she tossed her clothes to the side.

"I didn't tell you to get undressed," Kamal said. "You're going to have to be trained to listen." He pulled her in close and slipped one of the handcuffs around her wrist.

"I don't know where this is going, but I like it," she said with a grin.

Kamal finished cuffing her hands behind her, and then holding her shoulders, lowered her onto the blanket.

"We're not quite done," he said, pulling her hair into a ponytail. He then proceeded to tie her feet as well, so she couldn't run away.

"I feel . . . ready," she said playfully. "That's turning me on."

"That's the point," Kamal said. He slid his hand up and down her bare legs, stopping in the most sensitive places.

Kamal proceeded to touch, caress, and fondle her until she was practically writhing with excitement. The noise of ocean waves rose and fell as her breathing and moaning intensified.

By the time Kamal got undressed, she was practically begging him to finish. He paused for a moment, soaking in the control he had over her satisfaction.

Finally, twenty minutes after he had started, Kamal pulled her close and gave her what she had asked for, and then some. Her cries of ecstasy and passion were drowned out by the pounding waves.

• • • •

Kamal took a long draw on his cigarette, held it for a second, and exhaled slowly. He'd left the girl in a quivering puddle of exhaustion after going for almost an hour. He'd left her on the beach, tied up still, while he went to his car to clean up and grab a smoke. He grabbed a water bottle and a towel, then sighed. The crisp night air and crashing waves, combined with his physical exertion and a warm smoke, put him in a place of complete peace. Nothing else mattered at that point.

He was awakened an hour later by screaming.

Kamal jumped up and dashed down to the beach, fearing the worst. When he crested the dune, the girl was still there, naked and bound, squirming around. Three young men were standing around her in a circle, jeering at her while masturbating.

"Get the hell away from her!" Kamal shouted, breaking into a sprint. He narrowed the gap quickly, and before they could stop him, Kamal had punched one of them, causing the man to stumble back and fall, his pants still half undone.

The second man hastily zipped his pants up and managed to take off running. While Kamal was making sure the fallen man left, he heard a noise and turned, just in time to see the third man lock eyes with him.

Kamal froze, a slight smile growing on his face, until the third man exploded all over the girl's face with a shout.

Something about the whole situation just seemed funny to Kamal, and he started laughing. The man responded by laughing while zipping up his pants.

By the time Kamal had stopped laughing, he was alone with the girl again.

"They're finally gone!" the girl shouted, obviously still upset. She flopped around, trying to right herself.

"Calm down," Kamal said, still laughing quietly. "You're OK."

"Why did you leave me there? Couldn't you hear me calling for you?"

"Actually," Kamal said as he undid her restraints, "you were so good, I fell asleep."

Finally free, she pulled her hand back to slap Kamal, but stopped when he held his hands up.

"Look. I'll pay you double for putting up with them. They didn't hurt you, did they?"

"No. . ."

"OK then," Kamal chuckled as he pulled out his wallet. "Here you go."

The girl hesitated, but then grabbed the money, hastily put her clothes back on, and was gone.

Kamal just shook his head and grinned. "At least she'll remember me for a long time."

• • • •

"I thought I was going to die," Nicolette said.

Kamal's chin fell to his chest. Finding Nicolette awake and alert upon his return to Paris did not ease the guilt.

"So did I," he said. "It is my fault. All my fault. I am sorry. I thought I'd planned better—"

"Shh," Nicolette said as she reached a pale hand towards Kamal. "We did the best we could. We didn't know—"

"But I should have known" Kamal slid his fingers into hers. "I promise you . . . you will never be in danger again."

Nicolette began to pull back, but Kamal held on.

"How can you promise a thing like that? You are not God."

"No. But we cannot count on divine help. I learned that a long time ago. I can count on myself. On you." He squeezed Nicolette's hand tighter. She matched his pressure. "And you want to know something?"

"What? What is it?"

"You can count on me. And you can count on the new life we can create together."

"New life? What are you talking about?" Nicolette sat up straighter.

"This latest job . . . while you were asleep . . . it paid well. Very well. So well that before I came to see you, I made arrangements."

"How well?" Nicolette's eyes twinkled. "What arrangements?"

Kamal smiled.

"I have a surprise for you."

CHAPTER 9

RESTLESS

"You got something? For me?"

"Absolutely." Kamal turned back to Nicolette. She winced and rested a hand over her bandaged side.

Kamal handed her a postcard-sized photograph.

The photo offered an aerial view of a beautiful French villa, surrounded by hedges and rolling countryside. The sweeping arches lining the walkways drew her eyes to the large pool and courtyard beside it.

"I don't understand. Did you rent this for us?"

"No," Kamal said with a grin. "I bought it. It's your new home."

Nicolette's jaw dropped open, and she slowly shook her head. "Are you serious?"

"Yes. It's all paid for. We can go there as soon as the doctors release you."

"But why?" Nicolette, still amazed, looked into his eyes. "You didn't have to do all that."

"So you won't ever have to be in danger again." Kamal paused, taking a deep breath. "You can relax, and you won't have to work another day in your life."

"I—I don't know what to say!"

Kamal just smiled. "You don't have to say anything. Just accept it."

Nicolette leaned forward and wrapped her arms around Kamal. "Thank you," she whispered.

For only a second, Kamal felt peace, and drank it in deeply. And then, just like that, it was gone.

• • • •

It was only a matter of weeks before Kamal started noticing something was wrong.

"I'm going to sit on the patio!" Nicolette called from the kitchen.

Kamal didn't respond. He turned his attention back to the vegetables he was chopping, but something about Nicolette's tone of voice bothered him. It seemed flat, monotone. Bored and lifeless.

He put his knife down and followed Nicolette out into the courtyard patio, where the sun rippled across the surface of the pool. She was wearing a bikini and a large sun hat, and her eyes were hidden away with dark sunglasses. She strode casually to a lawn chair and sat down, leaning back into it like a familiar embrace. Her graceful form was lithe and as fit as ever.

Kamal stopped at the edge of the pool and sat, hanging his feet into the cool water.

"Are you OK, Nicolette?"

"Of course. Why would you ask that?" He lifted her sunglasses and gazed into her eyes.

"Something doesn't seem right." Kamal turned his head to her and shrugged. "There's something eating at you you're not telling me." He tightened his jaw. "I want you to tell me what it is."

"Ugh." Nicolette sighed and flopped back into the chair. "I hate it when you get that way."

"I'm serious. What's wrong? You have your own house in the French Riviera, in your name. You have your own convertible. You have everything you could ever want."

"I know," Nicolette said. "But I—I'm sorry. That's . . . the problem."

"Problem? That you have everything that anyone could ever dream of? That's the problem?"

"No! No, of course not." Nicolette laughed to calm Kamal. "I'm just . . . I'm just bored. Out of my mind. There's nothing to do but shop and sit at the pool and go out to eat." She pulled her sunglasses back over her eyes and sighed again. "I need some . . . excitement in my life."

"You mean almost dying?" Kamal grunted. "No. Absolutely not. I'm not going to let that happen."

"Then what's the point of living?" she snapped. "I want to feel alive again."

"But we don't have to steal anything ever again," Kamal countered. "We're set."

Nicolette didn't answer. After waiting long enough to know she wasn't going to, Kamal rose and went back inside. As he finished preparing dinner, he thought about what she'd said.

Nicolette needed excitement, but without danger. Maybe he could take her gambling? But that never excited her the way it did him. Maybe a cruise, or trip to the mountains.

Kamal remembered how excited Nicolette would get after each scam they would run. There was always a sense of accomplishment. In the end, she was just like him- always needing to find some kind of scheme to run—not for the money, but for the excitement.

• • • •

"Bonjour! How may I help you, sir?"

Kamal looked the man behind the counter up and down. He was dressed in a suit, conservatively, but with a touch of cut and color.

"I'm looking for a piece of jewelry for my lady friend. Something special." He turned and nodded towards Nicolette, who was across the room chatting with one of the sales ladies.

"Ah, yes, I see," the man nodded. "Does she prefer necklaces, earrings, or rings?"

"Let me see your necklaces. She likes to wear low dresses with something nice."

The clerk nodded. "Excellent. We have some wonderful choices over here. Chokers, pendants, matinee length . . . "

While they pored over the collection of diamond necklaces, the bell over the door tinged, and another customer walked in. He was a larger man, with a goatee and a bald head.

Kamal continued to let the salesman ramble on, but his ears picked up on something the big customer said to one of the other sales associates.

"Big event coming up. Are you going to be there?"

"Yes sir," the attendee at the counter said. "We're planning on having a table at the conference."

"Do you know where it is? I know they're holding it in Beirut in September, but I'm not sure what hotel."

Kamal snapped back to attention. "I'm sorry, what were you saying?"

"These necklaces right here," the clerk droned, "are all exquisitely designed around these valuable stones, which have each been certi-fied . . . "

Kamal's brain tuned out again as his mind raced. He finally held up a hand, interrupting the salesman. "Did he say there's a jewelry convention in Lebanon in about three months?"

"Um, er . . . yes, that's correct."

"Who would be there for that? What kind of pieces could I find there?"

The clerk's eyes lit up. "Ah, well, practically anything, really. Some of the biggest designers in the business will be there to reveal their new lines. And of course," he said with a smile, "dealers will be there selling and trading gemstones, including some of the biggest diamond moguls in the world."

"That sounds spectacular," Kamal mused, already narrowing down in his mind where a conference of this size could be held with enough security to attract international audiences. "Now about these necklaces . . . I'll take this one here, with the cameo."

"Ah yes, a classic design. Very nostalgic."

"I'm not big on nostalgia," Kamal commented, "but I know beauty when I see it."

• • • •

Kamal looked at the police officer, eyeing him up and down. "Can I ask you a favor?"

The officer, standing outside a hotel parking garage, acknowledged Kamal and nodded. "Depends."

"Can I ask you a few questions about the company running security for these big hotels?" Kamal cracked a big grin. "I'm writing a story for the paper on the working conditions they make you deal with."

"I can't really tell you much," the officer replied, relaxing noticeably. "We just do as we're told."

"I'm guessing they don't pay you very well, do they? Do they ever ask you to work long weekends with overtime?"

"Yeah, they do. Every now and then they'll have a big convention or something, and we'll have to work three or four days straight with little to no sleep."

"I heard there's a big thing coming up in Lebanon in a few months, do you know anything about it?" Kamal reached into his pocket and pulled out a roll of money. "I'm willing to pay for information."

The officer's face lit up. "Well, I know some of us are going to work a huge convention there, downtown, in about three months. We're not allowed to ask for vacation during that week."

"That's horrible!" Kamal said, feigning disgust. He placed the wad of bills in the guard's hand, and added, "What else can you tell me about this convention?"

· · · ·

"Welcome! How may I help you two?"

Kamal glanced at Nicolette, then turned to the front desk receptionist. "We're staying overnight for a business trip tomorrow. We'd like to go out somewhere nice this evening, but nothing too strenuous or far, as we have a long flight home tomorrow."

"Understood." He brightened his smile. "Is there anything else I can do for you?"

Nicolette nodded. "Do you have someplace where we can store our valuables while we're out for dinner?"

"Oh, most definitely," the man beamed. "We have security boxes for every suite. I'll have someone from the desk bring you a key before you leave."

Kamal smiled. "Perfect."

They arrived at the restaurant and had a wonderful dinner overlooking the ocean skyline at dusk. When they were finished eating, Nicolette leaned back and sighed.

"How do you like your Champagne?" Kamal asked, reclining in a leather chair.

"It's lovely," Nicolette answered, taking a sip from her glass. "Dinner was lovely, too."

"Are you ready for the fun part?"

Nicolette smiled. "Of course."

Kamal waved to the waiter, who approached.

"I trust your meal was to your liking?"

Kamal nodded. "Everything was perfect. We're ready to go."

"Of course," the waiter replied with a small bow. "I'll be right back."

The waiter returned and handed Kamal the check, and waited quietly. Kamal pulled out his wallet, handed the waiter some bills, and stood up, with Nicolette following suit.

"Enjoy the rest of your night!" the waiter chimed.

Kamal nodded as he and Nicolette walked out into the breezeway, where a black Mercedes was waiting. The driver stood at attention and smiled upon seeing them.

"Good evening. Where would you like to go?"

"I think we'll return to the hotel," Kamal replied.

"Very well," the chauffeur said, opening the door for them. They climbed in, and a few minutes later, were in front of the hotel.

With a tip to the driver, Kamal and Nicolette split up. While Nicolette walked through the hotel lobby, Kamal approached the desk where he was greeted by a tall, slim man.

"I'd like to retrieve my belongings," Kamal said, prompting the desk attendant to motion them around to a side hallway.

There, flanked by two guards, was the door to the hotel vault. He entered and turned to the left, where a side room, much like a post office, was lined with keyed boxes.

Kamal went to their room's safety box, opened it with a key, and retrieved a small container of money. He stuffed it into his pocket, then closed the safety box again.

He emerged from the vault, gave a nod to the guards, and made his way to the elevator, where Nicolette was waiting.

• • • •

After entering their suite, Nicolette spun around and flopped on the bed with a giggle.

"Are you excited, sweet Nicol? You sure you're not bored?"

"Not a bit," she laughed. "This is going to be fantastic."

"Good." Kamal went to his suitcase and pulled out a small machine, roughly the size of a small bench vice. He then pulled something out of his pocket.

"Here's the safety box key," he said. "And here's a blank. Would you like to watch?"

With a nod, Nicolette was up and watching over his shoulder. Kamal put the safe key in one side of the machine and clamped it in place. Then he did the same for the blank on the other side.

"The way it works is this. The pointer follows the key on the left, and guides the cutter on the right. So you get an exact copy."

"Does it make a lot of noise?"

"It kind of does, yes. But it only takes a minute to cut one." He raised an eyebrow. "Wouldn't you like to draw a nice soothing bath after our long night? I think that might work."

Nicolette grinned. "I'll get the water started."

• • • •

Over the next two months, Kamal and Nicolette alternated checking into the hotel in downtown Beirut every three to four days for an overnight stay. Each time, they would request a different suite, and spend the evening out. He made sure to make the reservations by phone and use a different name each time, so that if someone searched the records they wouldn't see a pattern. The only person in the hotel who saw the fake name was the clerk who handed out the room keys, and Kamal made sure to only minimally interact with him, so he wouldn't become too familiar.

For every visit they made to the hotel, Kamal and Nicolette would change their appearance completely. Everything from their hair, clothes, and luggage, to their mannerisms and accents. They made every effort to blend in and not draw attention to themselves.

After they had made twenty or so visits, Kamal had enough keys to finish his plan. By then, they had found out exactly who would be coming.

Weeks before the convention, Kamal made sure to book a suite to secure a spot. He had registered a jewelry business under a pseudonym, which was enough to gain entry to the convention if necessary.

By the weekend the convention was taking place, Nicolette's excitement was overflowing.

"This is going to be so much fun!" she said gleefully. "It feels like we've been planning this forever."

"I know," Kamal said. "But now is our shot. All we have to do is hang out, talk to people, and blend in. Then when they've shut everything down and people have turned in for the night, we go to the vault and clean it out."

Nicolette grinned widely. "I can't wait."

A few hours later, the hotel lobby and ground floor were filled with people milling about. There were more than a hundred people, including dealers and buyers, trying to make their way into the main ballroom.

Kamal and Nicolette squeezed their way past people arguing and chatting into the hall, where long tables spanning 100 feet on each wall were covered in shiny displays of gold and diamonds. Nicolette's eyes popped seeing so much wealth in one place.

"Just blend in . . . look around," Kamal said.

By that evening, they had looked at almost everything. Kamal was tired of being on his feet, and Nicolette looked like she was ready for a rest as well.

"OK," Kamal said once they had met back up. "We're going to make ourselves scarce while they pick up the tables. Some of the dealers brought their own vaults in vans to store their merchandise, but a lot of the smaller dealers won't have that."

"So should we go get dinner?" Nicolette yawned and stretched. "Then we can relax for a few. I'm going to need to take these shoes off."

"Good. Let's plan to stay out for a while."

"How late?"

"As late as we need to."

. . . .

When they returned that night, it was well after midnight. The hotel lobby had a few late night travelers, but all of the convention-goers had retired for the evening.

Kamal approached the front desk and spoke to the man behind the desk.

"Excuse me. I lost track of the time, and I still need to put away our things from the show. Is the vault still open?"

"Yes, it is," the man replied with a nod. "I'll make sure the vault stays open for you."

"Thank you, excellent." Kamal walked through the lobby once more, taking the elevator to their suite.

Minutes later, Nicolette reemerged with a large handbag, and headed to the hallway where the safebox storage room was.

"I'd like to get my jewelry to go out tonight," she said kindly to the security guard. He smiled and waved her inside. She had used that excuse many times before, and always made sure to put something on to sell the lie.

Wasting no time, Nicolette pulled out a keyring full of box keys, and slung her handbag on her shoulder.

"Let's see what we've got," she smiled. She opened the first security box, and to her surprise, found nothing.

Quickly locking it shut again, she frowned. "Well, I guess I knew they wouldn't all have something."

She then set to work, opening box after box as fast as she could, scooping the contents of each into her handbag. Cash, felt bags of diamonds, gold chains, whatever was inside.

"Are you about done in there, miss?"

Nicolette froze. "Yes," she called out quickly. "Just a second."

She mentally counted the keys she'd gone through—only about twenty-five. She looked wistfully at the boxes she hadn't gotten to, but decided that making it out with what she had was better than getting caught with everything.

Just as she was closing the box, the guard appeared.

"Oh!" Nicolette gasped. "You startled me!" She let out a little giggle.

"All done?" the guard asked plainly, eyeing her up and down.

"Yes." She casually pocketed the keys, and held up a necklace. "Do you think it would look good with this dress?" She held it up to her bosom and leaned forward, giving the guard a good look.

"Uh, yes ma'am," he stammered.

"Thanks." Nicolette turned and headed out of the secure area. As she passed the guard, she lowered her eyes and smiled slightly. The guard stared at Nicolette's butt as she sauntered down the hallway and into the night.

• • • •

"These are some wonderful gems. Where did you get these?"

Kamal sighed. It had been two weeks since they left the jewelry show in Beirut, but it had taken him that long to find someone who would fence the amount of diamonds he had.

"I bought them off of an estate sale in France."

The man grunted. "Must have been one hell of an estate. These are beautiful." He looked up at Kamal and removed the loop from his eye. "I can get you top money for these, no questions asked."

"That's the best kind of money," Kamal said with a wry smile. "The kind with no questions attached."

"We'll usually either re-mount these, or if they're big enough, cut them up. Sometimes they're worth more that way."

"How much can you pay me up front?"

The man chewed his lip. "I can give you about half of the total worth, those are the ones I know I can cut. The rest depends on what they go into."

"Do whatever you need to do," Kamal said.

"Will do," the man replied. He reached behind the counter, and counted off a stack of bills into Kamal's hand.

"That should do it," Kamal said. "Just call me when you're done with the rest."

With that, Kamal left the shop and jumped into his convertible parked outside. He started the car, dropped it into gear, and headed home.

• • • •

The next morning, Kamal woke and headed to the corner bistro for breakfast like he usually did. As Kamal drove, a noise snapped him out of his thoughts. It was the new car phone he'd just bought, courtesy of Al-Fahad. The sound finally registered after a second, and he picked it up.

"Al-Fahad."

"Hello!" Kamal answered. "What is it? I'm driving."

"I can hear you fine." There was a long pause.

"Kamal, I need to know if you were in Beirut two weeks ago."

Kamal hesitated.

"Uh, yes . . . I was. Nicolette and I were on vacation there as a matter of fact."

"Vacation. I'm sure. The reason I'm asking, Kamal, is that a good friend of mine was there as well."

"Is that right?"

"He was at this jewelry event. In Beirut. Someone there stole everything he'd brought with him, and robbed more than a dozen other individuals as well."

"That's really unfortunate."

"Kamal," Al-Fahad said. "You're the only man I know who can pull that off. It was you and the girl, Nicolette. Wasn't it?"

Again, Kamal held on to the silence.

"I don't need excuses," Al-Fahad snapped. "I know you didn't know. All I'm asking is that the item be returned, and all will be forgiven. I will even reimburse you its worth. This does not have to be messy."

Kamal felt his anger rising.

"That's going to be a problem. It's not going to happen."

"Problem?" Al-Fahad asked. "Why is that a problem?"

"Whatever jewel it was, it no longer is," Kamal said. "I had all the pieces cut and reset. Whatever your friend owned, he can't get it back."

"Perhaps I misspoke . . ." Al-Fahad said. "I'm not asking you. You will bring me that piece."

Then he hung up.

CHAPTER 10

FLIGHT

"**N**icolette, we're going to need to leave the country for a while." On the other end of the phone, there was nothing but silence.

"Are you there?" Kamal looked at the car phone and frowned.

After another few seconds, there was a reply.

"Yeah, I heard you. What's going on?"

"Don't worry about it," Kamal snapped. "We just need to get away for a while. I was thinking maybe a trip to Cairo. You know, Egypt . . . the pyramids . . . museums . . . plenty of sights to see . . ."

"Yes, I—I guess. It's just . . . sudden."

"Yes, but it's a surprise. A pleasant surprise." Kamal continued. "I'll make some calls, and we can leave tomorrow."

"Kamal . . ."

"Yes, Nicolette?"

"Is everything OK?"

"Yes," he said with a grimace. "Everything's fine. I'll help you pack when I get there."

He hung up the phone and returned his focus on steering the convertible through traffic as swiftly as he could. Kamal could feel his heart pounding, the same way it did when he was about to do something dangerous.

• • • •

Cairo was a massively busy place, even for someone like Kamal that had grown up in big urban sprawl. It reminded him of home. They had spent the morning walking around the shops and markets, looking at the usual trinkets and souvenirs.

Eventually, they made their way to the central part of the city, where they stumbled upon a museum of ancient Egyptian history.

The museum was filled with incredible artifacts from ancient Egypt, including jewelry, photographs of hieroglyphics, a sarcophagus and several statues. Some of the statues were giant, and some were no bigger than a handbag.

"This place is amazing!" Nicolette turned to Kamal and motioned him closer. "Look at the details on this statue."

But the one in particular that had caught Nicolette's eye was of an Egyptian deity—a lithe woman's body with a feline head.

"Who do you think this is a statue of?" Kamal asked, drawing in closer.

"I think it's either Bastet or Sekhmet." Nicolette examined the plaque next to it, and nodded. "Yeah, it's Bastet. It says she was the goddess of protection, fertility, and warfare."

Kamal chuckled. "No wonder you like it."

"Do you think we can get one like that?" Nicolette asked.

"You mean a souvenir?"

Nicolette grinned. "No. I mean a real one." She pointed to the statue again. "I could see that sitting on the mantle, looking out towards the sea."

Kamal raised an eyebrow. "Do you mean you want one of the ones here?"

She shot Kamal a sly grin.

Despite Nicolette's grin, Kamal shook his head. "No, I don't think even *I* could do that. But I'd be willing to bet there's a black market around here that I could find something at."

"You know where we could find one?"

Kamal smiled back. "I know some people."

• • • •

"Good day!" A large man with a beard and a turban greeted them as soon as they walked in the door. The building didn't look like much on the outside, but inside, the place was filled with colorful shelves of textiles, paintings, jewelry, and assorted odds and ends. "My name is Abumustafa, how may I be of service?"

Kamal cracked a broad smile. He hadn't seen that cheerful of a face in longer than he could remember.

"Same to you! I'm Kamal. How's business?"

"Things are going well. We've gotten a lot of merchandise recently." Abumustafa looked over at Nicolette, who was admiring some of the nicer necklaces on display. "I see you've got a friend with you, I don't think we've been introduced."

"I'm Nicolette." She nodded and returned his smile. "Kamal and I have been . . . friends for years."

"I see!" Abumustafa turned back to Kamal. "I'm sure you didn't drop by just because you were in the neighborhood. What can I help you with?"

"Nicolette here is enamored with statues of the Egyptian cat-goddess. I don't suppose you could find an authentic one?"

"I'm fairly certain I can find you one," Abu said. "Maybe not a large or famous one, but certainly. Bastet is very popular."

"Can you find one in good shape, about this big?" Kamal held his hands about a foot apart. "Something we can display."

"Let me see what I can find," Abu said, holding his hand up. "We should be able to locate something you'd like." Abu disappeared through a doorway, while Nicolette and Kamal waited.

"Kamal, you didn't have to do this," Nicolette said in a hushed tone.

"No, it's fine. I want to get you something nice that will give you good memories."

"Kamal . . ."

Just then, she was interrupted by Abumustafa returning walking through the door. "You're in luck!" Abu exclaimed. "We've got something I know you'll love, but it's at a warehouse across town."

"Can we come back later to pick it up?" Kamal asked. "We'll be in town for a few days."

"Yes, of course." Abu nodded, then sighed. "But getting it out of the country is going to be a bit of a trick. It's just that the customs officers will confiscate anything that looks remotely suspicious."

Kamal grinned. "We'll see about that."

• • • •

Kamal and Nicolette spent the afternoon sitting in a restaurant, enjoying the local delicacies as they chatted. When they were finished, Kamal decided it was time to go back to the market, to see if Abumustafa had received the statue.

When they arrived and stepped out of the cab, however, Abumustafa was standing outside, looking excited. As they approached, Abu glanced around and motioned them inside.

Abumustafa immediately brightened up. "I have good news! We managed to find this beauty for you . . ."

Abumustafa turned and pulled out an object wrapped in white linen cloth. "This particular piece was recovered from a tomb not far from Giza. I'm not sure who it belonged to, but it's an excellent example."

As he unwrapped the cloth, Nicolette's eyes lit up. Underneath was a statue of the Egyptian goddess Bastet. Standing, it was about 25 centimeters tall, and made of solid brass. The lithe female figure had its arms crossed, holding a staff and hook. The feline head was colored with meticulous painted detail. It had to be thousands of years old but at the same time felt timeless.

"That's perfect." Nicolette gushed. "I love it!"

"I'm very pleased you like it!" Abumustafa said with a smile. "This will be a wonderful addition to any collection." He turned to Kamal and loudly whispered, "It's almost as beautiful as her!"

"I agree," Kamal said. "How much is it?"

Abumustafa named a number, and Kamal pulled out his wallet.

Kamal thanked him and handed him some money, while Abu carefully re-wrapped the statue in a protective cloth. When it was finished, Kamal gathered the statue in his arms and brought it outside, where the cab was waiting. Nicolette followed excitedly.

As they loaded into the car, Abumustafa observed from a distance. "I hope you have a safe trip home," he said.

"Thank you," Kamal replied. "I expect we'll be OK, but I appreciate the help."

• • • •

"Pull over, this is perfect," Kamal shouted to the taxi driver, who quickly stopped the car.

"What are we stopping for?" Nicolette asked. "Shouldn't we be getting back to the hotel?"

"Not yet," Kamal said with a grin. "I want to pick up a souvenir first."

Stepping out of the car, he walked over to where a large storefront was festooned with banners and signs. It was a large chain store, the kind that popped up all over the city. He disappeared inside, and a few minutes later emerged with a large bag in his arms. After dodging a few red-and-white buses, he dashed across the street to where the cab was waiting.

"What did you get?" Nicolette asked with some curiosity as he climbed back into the taxi. "Anything for me?"

"Sort of," Kamal replied. "We're going to need this later." He reached in and pulled out a large statue of the Sphinx, and placed it in his lap.

"Driver?" Kamal tapped the man on his shoulder. "Can you take us to the arts district?"

The driver nodded, and wheeled the car out into the street, headed towards the center of town.

• • • •

"Why are we in a crafts store?" Nicolette's enthusiasm was clearly waning.

"We need some supplies here," Kamal replied. "You see those plaster statues over there?"

Nicolette nodded. "Yes. They look like cartoon animals. For children."

"Yes," Kamal said, "they're made with simple plaster and molds."

As they were looking at the plaster figurines, a woman approached them with a smile. "Can I help you?"

"Yes," Kamal said quickly. "I'd like to make some plaster figures for a relative, but I'm not sure what I'd need."

"Do you have a mold already?"

"No," Kamal said thoughtfully. "I was thinking about making a copy of something."

"Ah, yes," the woman nodded. "You'll want to make a mold. I have the materials for that." She motioned towards the wall, where racks of jars were stacked. "We've got some silicone, some resin . . ."

After a discussion on types of mold material, Kamal ended up buying some silicone, plaster, and a handful of paints. The shopkeeper insisted he grab a small booklet on how to use the materials, for which Kamal was grateful.

As they left the shop and made their way back to the hotel, Nicolette gave Kamal a playful look. "This seems like a lot of trouble to go through to get a statue through customs."

"It might seem that way," Kamal quipped, "but you know the real reason I'm doing it."

"For me?" Nicolette smiled.

"For you."

. . . .

"I still don't see anybody." Nicolette pulled back the curtains one more time, scanning the courtyard for anyone suspicious. "Is there someone specific I should be looking for?"

"No," Kamal said. "Just watch for someone who doesn't look like they're a hotel guest." He chuckled a little. "You know. Like we used to do."

That brought a smile to her face. Nicolette turned and sighed. "I do kind of miss those days."

"They were exciting, that's for sure." Kamal finished unwrapping the statues and plaster supplies, and spread them out on the table. "But if we can't work things out with Al-Fahad, those days will be nothing compared to what could happen."

"What are you going to do?"

"What we're going to do," Kamal said with a wave of his hand, "is basically use this Sphynx souvenir to make a mold. Then we're going to use that mold to make a duplicate statue around the real one. We'll seal the real one in plastic so it won't be damaged. Once that's done, we can make the plaster copy around it using the mold."

Kamal pulled out a cardboard box, roughly the size of a microwave oven. Using the buckets of mold silicone, he filled the box halfway, and then carefully lowered the Sphinx statue he'd bought earlier into it.

"Now we wait until that half is cured, and I can pour the other half."

"Can we go get something to eat in the meanwhile?"

"Absolutely," Kamal said. "I haven't tried the local Kushari yet."

• • • •

"Are you ready to head back home?" Kamal asked, holding out his hand to help Nicolette out of the car. She emerged, looking like she'd just come from a beach resort. She was wearing a crop top and short shorts to attract just enough attention.

"I'm more than ready," she replied. "Egypt is nice to visit, but I much prefer France."

They grabbed their bags and headed for the main lobby of the airport, where people were coming and going busily. They made their way through the crowds until they reached the terminal, where the row of ticket booths was.

As Kamal approached the counter, Nicolette tapped him on the shoulder.

"Kamal, I think that man's following us."

Kamal glanced in the direction Nicolette was looking. There was a crowd of people milling around, and trying to spot the motion of a single person proved difficult.

"Possibly," Kamal replied. "Just keep an eye on him. I don't think he'll cause any trouble here."

Nicolette nodded. The two of them walked around the ticket booths to where the main entrance to the terminal was. There were three security guards there, checking people's bags as they passed through.

As they approached security, Kamal flashed Nicolette a smile. She nodded, and seeing the guards, immediately turned on her charm.

"Bonjour!" she cooed, causing the guard next to her to just stare for a second. It had the intended effect, as the guard barely managed to form a complete sentence as he waved her through. Kamal followed quickly behind, hoping to not be noticed.

"I need to search your bag," the guard barked as Kamal stepped through the gate.

"Excuse me?"

The guard pulled Kamal aside, away from the line. "Put your bag up on this table," he instructed.

Kamal's heart raced, but he did as he was told. The guard proceeded to unzip and open the bag, dumping the contents out onto the table for everyone to see. Almost immediately, the Sphinx statue they were trying to smuggle tumbled out with a thud.

"Careful with that souvenir!" Kamal snapped. The guard ignored him, but examined it anyway. Seeing nothing obvious, he dumped the contents back into the bag and shoved it back towards Kamal.

"You can go on through."

Breathing a sigh of relief, Kamal gave the guard a nod, and strode through the first gate, where Nicolette was waiting anxiously.

"Did they suspect anything?" she asked.

"I don't think so," Kamal answered. "He probably just didn't like the way I looked."

"I think we're good!" Nicolette giggled. "They don't have a clue."

"That's what I love about you," Kamal said with a wry grin. "You love the thrill."

Nicolette threw an arm around his neck, and gave him a kiss on the cheek. "I wouldn't have anything if it weren't for you."

They continued through the hallway until they reached a wide part of the terminal. There were several shops set up, and benches for travelers to rest. Kamal sat down on one of the benches, his back to the wall, and dropped his carry-on luggage bag next to him. Nicolette decided to go get something to drink while they waited for their plane to board.

While she was occupied, Kamal actively scanned the people passing by from his vantage point. He didn't think he was in danger, insomuch as Al-Fahad probably had people keeping tabs on where they went. He was going to have to deal with that problem eventually, but for now, there wasn't anything he could do about it.

A few minutes later, Nicolette returned with a worried look on her face. There was another officer walking beside her, holding her by the elbow.

"I'd like you to come with me," the officer said. "We need to ask you two some questions." He glanced at Kamal. "You're with her, correct?"

Kamal nodded. "Yes, we're from France. We have boarding passes— we just need to find the gate and get on when they call for boarding."

"I insist," the officer said, a little more forcefully. "Come with me, please. We need you to make a statement."

"We're going to miss our flight!" Nicolette said hotly. "We don't have time for this!"

"Madame," the officer said, "I'm not asking you." He glared at Kamal, patted his gun holster, then motioned. "You too. Come with me, this way."

Nicolette shot Kamal a glance, but there wasn't much they could do to argue. Kamal picked up their bags and followed the officer through the terminal until they reached an area that was off of the main hallway.

"Through here, please," the officer said, pointing to a door. He stepped forward and opened it, gesturing inside.

As they entered, Kamal could make out a narrow hallway lined with rooms, each with a large window, with chairs and tables visible inside. It looked kind of shabby, and smelled like cigarette smoke.

"In here please," the officer said. He opened the door to the first room and waited until they were both inside, then closed the door behind them without entering.

And then Kamal heard the door lock with a clack.

They were trapped.

• • • •

For the next hour, every minute passed slowly as possible. Kamal's mind worked through scenario after scenario, trying to account for every possible contingency. In the end, they just had to wait.

Eventually, it was Cairo police, not airport security, that showed up. The door unlocked and swung open, revealing a pair of policemen.

"I'm sorry for the delay," one officer said. "We've gotten a report that someone was trying to smuggle a restricted item through the airport, and you two match the description."

"We're just here from Paris, on vacation." Kamal pulled his passport out of his pocket and handed it to the officer.

"Anton Ledet?" The officer said, flipping it closed again. "You don't look like a Ledet."

"How rude!" Kamal snorted. "I beg your pardon. I have never, in all my life, been treated so poorly!" He glared at the two men, doing his best to hide his fear. If they caught on, he wouldn't be going anywhere except to jail.

"And yours?" The officer said, nodding at Nicolette.

"Unbelievable!" she hissed as she pulled her passport from a pocket in her bag. "Why are you treating *me* like a criminal?"

"Michelle Bourgeois, is it?" The man tossed the passport onto the table back towards her. "Where are you coming from?"

"I expect an apology before I do anything!"

"We're still going to have to search you." The second officer stepped over and grabbed Nicolette's bag, prompting her to slap his hand away.

In an instant, Kamal was on his feet, bristling. In a flash, the first officer stepped in between them.

"No, no! That won't be necessary." The officer held his hand out, motioning Kamal to sit down again, while the second officer glared at him.

"We can make this quick," he added, "or we can make this difficult. I don't want to have to file more paperwork than I need to." The officer pointed to their bags. "We are going to have to search these if you want to leave. If you have nothing to hide, this shouldn't be a problem." His face darkened. "This is *not* up for discussion."

The second officer sneered at Kamal. "You'd better listen. We're not playing around. Your girl here, though . . ."

"Enough," the first officer snapped. "Empty your bag contents on the table."

Nicolette sighed and lifted her bag onto the table, unzipped it, and began pulling out clothes. When she pulled out a handful of bikinis, the annoying guard snickered, but kept his mouth shut.

Finally, she had emptied everything, and with a smirk, held the bag upside-down to prove there was nothing left, and then dropped it on the table.

The officer pulled out a knife and proceeded to cut apart the inside of the bag with long slices, revealing layers of thin padding, but nothing more.

"Very well," the officer said. "Pack it back in. Sir, Mr. Ledet, if you don't mind?"

As Nicolette stuffed her things back into the now ruined suitcase, Kamal heaved his up onto the table, unzipped it, and flipped the top open.

There, sitting on top of everything, was a statue of the Sphinx, about two feet long.

Kamal shrugged. "We were sightseeing. What did you expect?"

The officer held out his hand, as a warning for Kamal not to move. "Let's see what we've got here. I'll decide whether or not you're clear." He pulled the statue from the suitcase and laid it on the table.

Kamal's irritation grew, but he said nothing.

The officer then reached into his pocket and pulled out his knife again, and flicked it open.

Every nerve in Kamal's body screamed for him to lash out and fight, but with deep breaths, he forced himself to slow his heart rate and look a little more relaxed.

The officer took the knife blade and stabbed the statue right in the middle, knocking out a small chunk of resin. Kamal looked carefully to see if the statue underneath had been revealed, but he couldn't quite tell.

The officer continued to chip away at the statue in several places, each time taking a chunk out of it, but never going too deep. The cheap material chipped off here and there, showing spots of color underneath.

Kamal took a deep breath, hoping that was the end of it, but with a pop, the resin casing split in half, and the carefully wrapped Bastet figurine, wrapped in plastic, fell out onto the table.

Kamal began to make some sort of excuse, but before he could get a word out, he was interrupted by the ringing of a cell phone.

The guard reached into his pocket and flipped open the phone. "Hello?" Kamal's brow began to bead with sweat. This was definitely not going as planned.

Suddenly, the guard nodded and held the phone out to Kamal.

"It's for you, Mr. Kamal."

Stunned, Kamal's jaw dropped. He forced himself to take the phone and hold it up to his head.

"Kamal, where are you going in such a rush?" The voice was unmistakable. Al-Fahad. "Were you thinking of taking a vacation?"

"No! I wasn't trying to . . ."

"Don't play games with me, my young friend." Al-Fahad's voice had taken on an uncharacteristically grave tone. "If I wanted to hurt you, I would have. Do you understand?"

"I understand." Kamal frowned.

"This isn't over." The phone went dead.

Kamal's face went pale, and he glanced at Nicolette. Her eyes grew wide.

The guard retrieved the phone, and gave a short bow. "I apologize for the inconvenience," he began. "We've been ordered to release you both. You're free to go." As Kamal stood and began to close his bag, the captain added, "We're letting you go with a warning."

Kamal gave him a frown. "I suppose I should be thankful." He slung the suitcase around and lowered it to the floor, while Nicolette swung her bag over her shoulder.

They exited the office and walked back out into the terminal, which was now lit up with lights, as night had fallen.

"Just lovely," Nicolette said. "What else could go wrong?"

"Don't say things like that," Kamal retorted. "You know how I feel about it."

"You're right," she acknowledged. "I'm sorry. Can we just go home now?"

"I hope so," Kamal sighed. "I really hope so."

• • • •

Morning dawned in Paris as Kamal and Nicolette found their way out of the airport to a taxi. Next was a short trip to long-term parking where Nicolette's car was parked. Neither had gotten much sleep on the plane. Nicolette would need to catch up as soon as they arrived home, if not sooner.

Kamal took the driver's side of Nicolette's convertible.

"Kick off your shoes," he said. "Get some sleep."

Nicolette, exhausted and unkempt, mumbled a yes. She was buckled in and asleep before they left the parking lot.

Kamal had a phone call to make. The engine's hum and Nicolette's gentle snore told Kamal it was time. International mobile calls cost a fortune, but this could not wait for the landline.

"Al-Fahad."

The man picked up after half a ring.

"Did you receive my message?" Al-Fahad said without greeting.

"Yes, I did, as a matter of fact." Kamal said. He took a deep breath to steady his voice. "Loud and clear."

"You need to understand," Al-Fahad said, "that you will never be safe if you try to run from me. You see that now, yes? It doesn't matter where or how, I will find you and destroy you."

"I *am* sorry for what happened," Kamal said as calmly as possible. His heart was pounding. His vision blurred. "There's not much I can do about it now, but I'll do my best to make this right. This was all a misunderstanding."

"I need to resolve this situation, one way or another," Al-Fahad said. "The debt must be paid. I let her go unharmed this time, but I cannot guarantee it in the future."

Kamal glanced over at Nicolette, and his heart sank. "I think I understand," he replied. All kinds of horrible things passed through his mind, but he shoved them aside. "Will you at least give me a chance to make it right?"

"I will give you . . . hmm . . . two weeks. Yes, two weeks to fix this. Do not disappoint me."

"I'll take care of it," Kamal said. He checked Nicolette out of the corner of his eye—still asleep.

Al-Fahad hung up without another word. Kamal realized there was only one way he was going to be able to be a free man again.

CHAPTER 11

RECKONING

The streets of Paris were full of people bustling about, as usual. Kamal made his way through the crowd, weaving through throngs of people, until he reached an intersection. He had two weeks to come up with a plan before his meeting with Al-Fahad. Lebanon wasn't safe, and the house in France was surely being monitored. It would be hard to make things go in his favor.

As he stood there at the crosswalk waiting to cross the street, Kamal noticed people pointing and looking. Craning his neck, he could make out that a portion of the street was blocked off.

He turned and approached the barricades, for a moment forgetting his errands. He pressed into the crowd, hoping to catch a glimpse of what lay beyond.

He saw what looked like a crime scene—police, a coroner, caution tape, and emergency vehicles—except for one thing. There were cameramen with large studio cameras on their shoulders capturing the entire thing.

Seconds later, someone yelled, "Cut! That's a take!" And all the policemen turned and walked away, leaving the cameramen talking amongst themselves. And then, to Kamal's surprise, a covered dead body sat up, pulled the covering off, and stood up.

They were filming a show. The official-looking people, including the policemen, were all actors.

Kamal smiled and turned to leave. As he strolled down the street, a plan started to form. Two weeks was just enough time to do what he needed. It would send him back to Cairo, but there was money to be made in Cairo anyway.

• • • •

"I'd like to rent out one of the office buildings in this new industrial park."

The woman looked at Kamal. "You said you're a director?"

"I am, yes. From France. Here is my license." Kamal smiled and turned towards her. "I've got a fantastic script for a show, I have the funds to hire the crew and actors. I just need a spot to film it. The building is new, and this district outside Cairo is a perfect backdrop."

The complex they were standing in front of was freshly painted, and still had some construction materials stacked in the parking lot.

"We require a deposit of three month's rent," the woman answered. "Can you do that?"

"Absolutely," Kamal shot back. "When can I start moving in?"

"Electrical is hooked up and ready."

"Fantastic. I'm going to need a few days to get everything together. We have a contract then."

"Yes, yes. Thank you." She nodded. "Just sign the lease papers, and write out the check. We'll get everything sorted." She handed him a metal clipboard and a pen.

"Perfect." Kamal grabbed the pen and scribbled on the paper where required, and handed them back to the woman.

After the woman checked everything was done, Kamal went back to his car, left the office, and drove back to the center of town. There was still a lot to do, including calling the talent agency. But first, he had something more important to tend to.

He picked up his car phone as he drove, and punched in some numbers. "Hello?"

"Hey, this is Kamal. Were you able to find what I asked for?"

"Yes sir," the voice responded. "I'll have it for you when you get here."

"I'm on my way." Kamal wheeled the car around a turn and headed towards downtown Cairo. He had figured he'd need to bribe someone to get him government tax records, but he hadn't expected it to be so easy.

A few minutes later, he pulled up to a parking lot outside the government records building, and stepped out of his car. A middle-aged man spotted Kamal and approached him, holding a briefcase.

"Are you Kamal?" The man asked.

"I am. Does that briefcase have copies of the reports I need?"

The man nodded. "All tax filings from companies over one hundred employees that haven't been audited in the last five years."

"Perfect," Kamal said. He pulled an envelope from his pocket and handed it over. "Here's your fee, plus a little extra."

The man quickly flipped the envelope open, checked the contents, and smiled. "Thank you for your business," he added, handing the briefcase over to Kamal.

Kamal likewise checked the briefcase, and then tossed it into his car. "My pleasure." He started to turn, but then paused. "I suppose I shouldn't have to say it, but . . . "

"I have a family to feed on a government salary," the man replied. "I'm not going to risk that."

Kamal nodded. "Good." He jumped back into his car and took off without another word.

• • • •

Three days later, the set was ready. Kamal stood in the main office, making sure everything had been put in place, and each actor knew what to do. Nicolette had taken on the role of Kamal's secretary, and had been keeping an eye on things when he had his back turned.

"Remember," Kamal said to the group. "Don't break character. The cameras are hidden, so the contestants won't know they're part of the show yet." He glanced around, making sure everyone was paying attention. "Understood?"

The group, made up of twenty-one people, nodded. Nine were dressed as police officers, and the rest as office professionals.

"OK. The first contestant will be here in a few minutes. When the door opens, follow the script. If you see anything out of place, tell my assistant," he added, pointing to Nicolette.

Each person took their position. A few actors and two of the officers headed down to the main entrance. Kamal followed them down to the lobby, where a receptionist's desk and some potted plants had been installed. He motioned for the officers to take their places, and then headed up to his office.

A few minutes later, a limousine slid up to the entrance, and a tall, thin man in a suit stepped out. He looked around briefly, then entered the building.

The lobby opened into a waiting area, where Nicolette was pretending to be the main receptionist. Nicolette looked up and smiled. "May I help you?"

"Yes, I was asked to meet someone here from the government. A Mr. Adel?"

"Do you have an appointment?" Nicolette asked flatly.

"My name is Talal. I was contacted by the State Department to come to this address, on this day," he insisted. "They never mentioned a time."

"I see." Nicolette looked through some papers, then back at the man. "His office is on the second floor, the elevator's over there." She pointed with her pen.

When it was clear Nicolette wasn't going to continue the conversation, the man walked to the elevator and took it to the second floor, where the office area had been furnished. As he exited, the office workers glanced up, but quickly returned to their assigned roles.

The man looked around for any kind of sign that would indicate where the main office would be, and in frustration, eventually walked to the corner of the room where the biggest door was.

The office door was open, and as Mr. Adel looked in, he saw Kamal sitting behind a large desk, framed by a large window.

Kamal stood, smiled, and held his hand out. "Mr. Talal? I'm Adel. I'm the head of the Egyptian Tax Authority. I've been expecting you."

Mr. Talal nodded and shook Kamal's hand. "You could have told them I was coming. This is a new building?"

"Yes, that's correct," Kamal replied. "We're still working on getting everything moved, but the core staff is here. Sorry about the inconvenience." He motioned for Mr. Talal to have a seat, then sat as well.

"Please, let's talk. I know you're a busy man," Kamal said.

"I didn't want to come," Mr. Talal said flatly. "But it didn't seem like a trivial matter."

"Oh, most certainly, it's not. In fact," Kamal added, pushing a folder towards Mr. Talal, "if you look through these, you'll see it's a serious matter."

The man flipped open the folder, read a few sentences, and slapped it shut again.

"I understand you've been in the business of imports, is that right?"

"Yes . . . "

"Have you been audited recently, by any chance?"

Mr. Talal shook his head. "Why would I?"

"We've caught wind that you've been relabeling products illegally—specifically, relabeling cans of cat food as potted meat."

"It's basically the same thing," Talal said. "No one's complained."

"The product doesn't meet human consumption standards. But that's not my problem. That's the concern of the Ministry of Health and Population." Kamal frowned. "My problem is the profit you made. You have a government contract that says one thing, but you did another."

Mr. Talal crossed his arms. "Are you going to make an investigation, waste taxpayer funds, for this?"

Kamal showed the slightest hint of a smile. "We don't necessarily have to."

Talal sat up a bit straighter. "I'm not sure what you mean."

"Because of our office moving, this copy of your profile with all the evidence we've assembled, is the only copy we have." He tapped his finger on the folder. "How much do you think that's worth to your business?"

Talal raised his eyebrows. "Is that correct?"

Kamal nodded. "If this folder is still on my desk by Monday morning, I'm required to send it straight to Khalil Youssef, head of the Egyptian

Tax Authority." He paused. "Unless, I make it go away." Kamal's stare burned into Talal. "I can make *all kinds* of things go away."

Talal looked down at the folder, then back up to Kamal, and swallowed.

"How much are we talking here?"

"You've got a good bit to lose if this gets out," Kamal said. "It would affect all of your businesses, not just imports."

"Do you have a number in mind?"

"I was thinking a nice round number, like 500 hundred thousand dollars, would slide through recordkeeping pretty easily." Kamal leaned forward and folded his hands. "Let's be frank here. This is an opportunity to save everyone the headache of dealing with an investigation amid the freezing of your assets. Then there's the travel ban placed on you until the case is clear."

Mr. Talal said nothing.

"I can see you're an intelligent man," Kamal said. "I'm fairly certain you'll make the right choice."

"What account do you want me to transfer the money to?"

"Wire the money to this bank account," Kamal said, handing him a note. "When it clears, I will get a phone call, and this folder will be accidentally lost in the office move. You're free to do what you wish with it."

Mr. Talal chewed his lip for a moment, then nodded. "May I use your phone?"

· · · ·

As Kamal waited in his office, he chuckled to himself. He had taken the tax reports, found three companies with the biggest tax discrepancies, and told them they were in big trouble with the government. They were already going to be investigated by the State, but the way things worked in Egypt, if you paid someone off, they would look the other way. Kamal simply believed that there was no reason he couldn't be the one they gave their money to, as the State didn't need it.

Right on schedule, the second businessman showed up. Kamal was waiting for him, and gave him the same introduction that he had before.

"Mr. Mohamed! Welcome, I've been expecting you."

The rotund Mr. Mohamed grunted. "I hope you're not wasting my time."

"That remains to be seen," Kamal said. "I'd like to discuss it with you in my office."

Once in his office, Kamal closed the door behind him, and took a seat.

"Mr. Mohamed, how long have you been in the imports business?"

Mohamed fidgeted a little. "I took over a shipping company last year." He looked around nervously. "I'm not responsible for what they did before I bought them!"

"I understand that. What I'm more concerned with," Kamal said, sliding over a folder similar to the one he'd given Talal, "is what you've been doing with these shipments from China."

Cautiously, Mohamed opened the folder and read the front page. His face quickly turned red and he began to scowl. "What is the meaning of this?"

"As you can see here," Kamal said smoothly, "We've got records that you accepted an order for three million worth of wheat flour from the United States for use in industrial feed manufacturing."

Mohamed squirmed uncomfortably.

"Here, I can see you received a shipment of waste material from China, which surprisingly," Kamal added with a gesture, "is exactly the same amount as the government contract you bid on. And the dates somehow line up."

"I have documentation for those orders!" Mohamed stammered. "How dare you!"

Kamal held his hands up. "I understand your frustration. But what you see here," he said, pointing to the folder, "is the only existing copy of this report. How much would it be worth for me to make it disappear?"

"This is extortion!" Mohamed fumed, jumping to his feet. "I'll have nothing to do with this!"

"I don't think you understand," Kamal said calmly. "This report is going to end up at the head of the Egyptian Tax Authority. Look at it," he emphasized. "We've already got enough to tie your assets up in litigation."

Kamal reached over and hit a button on his desk phone. "Can you send security up to my office please?"

Mohamed froze. "What do you think you're doing?"

"I can put you under arrest for fraud, misbranding, and more than a dozen cases of poisoning." Kamal shrugged. "Or this report can go away."

Seconds later, the door burst open and the two security guards entered, causing Mohamed to back away slowly.

"Is everything OK?" the first guard asked.

"I'd like for you to stay outside my office for . . . safety reasons." Kamal motioned to Mr. Mohamed. "Mr. Mohamed here is feeling uneasy. I'll call you if I need you."

"Yes sir." The guards stepped outside and closed the door behind them.

"Mr. Mohamed, I don't want to deal with this mess any more than you do." Kamal tapped the folder again. "You should seriously consider it."

Mohamed sat down, his forehead covered in sweat. "I don't want to go to jail."

Kamal nodded. "That's good. I don't want you to go to jail, either."

"OK." Mohamed sighed deeply. "What do I have to do?"

• • • •

"In this report right here, Mr. Al-Aziz, is proof your company sold meat unfit for consumption, and labeled it misleadingly." Kamal looked intently at the man sitting across from him.

Mr. Al-Aziz was short, with a round face and straight hair. He looked at Kamal with disbelief. "Meat is meat, isn't that right?"

"Not according to the Ministry of Health." Kamal crossed his arms. "You can't sell donkey meat as beef."

"No one cares," Al-Aziz said. "They keep buying it, so it must taste good."

"*I* care. But everything we've documented that you've done is in this folder. This is the only copy." Kamal's voice was almost soothing.

"I suppose you'll offer me the chance to buy it from you?"

"That sounds like a reasonable suggestion," Kamal said smoothly.

"I have one question," Al-Aziz said, lowering his voice.

"What's that?"

"What's stopping me from taking your job from you?" Al-Aziz shifted slightly in his chair. "I know people who can do it."

Kamal's eyes widened, but his smile quickly returned. "I suppose you could. But let's say you did." Kamal pointed to the folder. "You would be not only arrested for fraud, but also for . . . something much worse."

"Possibly."

Kamal shook his head. "I have everything on you, right here in this folder."

Al-Aziz nodded. "That's also a possibility. But it could also be a bluff."

"Surely, a man as successful as yourself would know the odds. Let's see here . . ." Kamal opened the folder and flipped through some of the pages.

"Ah yes, look here. Your factory was also investigated for health code violations, which mysteriously disappeared- along with the investigator's wife." He slowly flipped the page. "And here, a photo of you and, is that your wife in the bikini?" Kamal looked up and smiled. "No, I don't think it is." He turned the page again. "I can keep going."

"What do you want from me?" Al-Aziz spat.

"All I'm asking is that you cut your losses." Kamal looked at the folder, then back up at Al-Aziz. "You've been careless. You're going to lose something regardless."

Al-Aziz just stared, his gaze as hard as steel.

"My offer will cause the least amount of pain for everyone involved." Kamal shrugged. "I'm sure you can see that, yes?"

Al-Aziz visibly relaxed, but his eyes didn't blink. "I think I understand."

"All I'm asking is that you make everybody's life easier." Kamal reached out with his hand and pushed the folder towards Mr. Al-Aziz.

"What's your price?"

"If you hadn't threatened me, it would have been lower, I'll be honest." Kamal grinned. "But I'm not an unreasonable man. A million sounds acceptable to make all this go away."

If Al-Aziz was surprised, Kamal couldn't tell. "I can do that," Al-Aziz said quietly. "But I'm not paying you cash."

"No need, no need," Kamal assured him. "A bank routing number should be enough."

As Al-Aziz placed the call, Kamal sighed. There was still a lot to do.

• • • •

"OK everyone, good job. That's a wrap for today."

Kamal waved his hands and gestured for everyone in the office to gather. "I've got good news. You've all been doing a great job, and we should have the footage we needed for the pilot by the end of the week. We have all your contact information, and we'll be in touch when the show gets greenlit."

One of the actresses raised her hand. "When will we get paid?"

"You'll be paid at the end of shooting this week." Kamal pointed to Nicolette, who was standing behind him. "See my assistant to pick up cash payment on Friday. You can keep any costume pieces we bought for you."

Kamal looked around and smiled. Everything had gone according to plan, even with a few hiccups. By the end of the week, the wire transfers would have cleared, and he would be a very wealthy man. But now the difficult part of the plan began—the part he wasn't looking forward to.

An hour later, Kamal and Nicolette were blasting west on the highway back towards the airport. The sun was setting, and the desert night air was beginning to chill.

As he drove, Kamal took a deep breath.

"Nicolette, I have a favor to ask of you."

"I have a question for you too. How much did we clear?"

"About 2 million dollars."

Nicolette gasped. "Are you serious?!"

"It was too easy. But about the airport . . ."

"Are you going back home?" she asked.

"I am, yes." Kamal looked wistfully into the distance. "I do have to make one more stop in Lebanon before I can meet back up with you."

"Kamal?"

"Yes, Nicolette?"

There was a pause. "Please be safe. If something happens . . ."

"I know, Nicolette. I know."

Nicolette cleared her throat. "Are you coming back to France?

"That's what I wanted to talk about. Things are very tense in Lebanon right now. I think it would be best for you to go to Greece."

"I suppose that's fine," she replied. "Is there anything you need me to do?"

Kamal bit his lip. "Just blend in with the tourists and stay out of sight until I get there."

. . . .

When Kamal stepped off the plane in Beirut, the smell immediately brought him back to his childhood. The ocean air, the food, and everything was just as he'd remembered it.

Kamal walked past the baggage claim into the lobby, and out into the parking lot. A brief jaunt later, and he'd reached where his car was parked in the parking garage. The package he'd ordered was on the passenger seat floorboard, just as he'd requested.

He jumped in, fired up the engine, and slapped the car in gear. Within minutes, he was free of the airport and heading away from the center of town.

Kamal wasn't sure how he ended up in front of the old Orphanage. He'd been driving around the seafront, and had taken a shortcut to get back to his condo. Maybe his brain just knew the area so well, he had ended up there subconsciously.

As if on cue, memories of his childhood there flooded his mind. Faces, laughter, tears, all flashed in front of Kamal's eyes. Two faces in particular caught his attention—Amir, who Kamal had watched die of poisoning, and another young boy, Mohammed. Kamal had called him "Mo" since the day they had met.

The place hadn't changed much in the last few years. On a whim, Kamal pulled his car through the gate and parked.

Approaching the office, Kamal could see younger children running around barefoot, like he remembered doing. He had been sending money to the orphanage for years, in hopes that it would help the children there not end up living on the streets like he had. Seeing it again was bittersweet.

Before he had reached the door, it swung open and a young woman, about 30, appeared. She smiled, and then seeing Kamal's face, broke into a wide grin.

"Kamal! Now there's a face I thought I'd never see again!"

He froze for a second. "You know me?"

"Of course," she said. "I remember. I was here then, too."

Kamal thought for a second. "And now you work here?"

"Absolutely! I love taking care of the children. When the director passed away, we went through a handful of people, but it was my calling to return here."

He smiled back at her. "Do you remember a boy we called Mo?"

She nodded. "He still lives in this area, actually. Across town. I saw him there a few weeks ago."

Kamal raised an eyebrow. "Can you tell me what street you saw him on?"

• • • •

Kamal looked the house over. It was run-down, dirty, and missing a few things, like most of the other houses in the poorest part of town.

After double-checking the number, Kamal approached the door and knocked firmly. There was some banging and shouting from inside, and he heard a voice yell "Come in!"

Kamal twisted the doorknob, and swung the door open with a creak.

Kamal entered and looked around. With the curtains closed, there wasn't much light to see. The walls were dingy. The carpet smelled of alcohol and was worn through in places. The only furniture was a mattress in the corner, half of a worn leather sectional sofa, and a coffee table. A large hookah sat atop the table, still full of smoke. He could faintly hear a radio in the background. Everything was covered in a layer of brown haze and dust.

There, sitting on the sofa, wearing nothing but boxer shorts, was Kamal's old friend, Mo.

"Can I help you?" Mo grunted.

Kamal held his breath for a second. "Hey, Mo. It's me, Kamal. Been a long time."

"Wait." Mo stood up and slowly walked towards Kamal, squinting.

"No way!" Mo paused, then broke into a wide smile. "It really is! You're the last person I expected to see at my door, man! I thought something had happened to you, I thought you were dead!" His speech was slow and slightly slurred. "I didn't think I'd ever see you again in this lifetime, man."

"Is this a bad time?" Kamal asked. "I can come back later."

Mo shook his head. "No, man, not at all, come on in!" He held his arms out wide. "It's not much, but this is my home."

Kamal wasn't quite sure what to say.

"Sit down," Mo insisted. "I'll be honest, I missed you, Kamal. Haven't seen your face in years! It's like seeing a ghost."

Kamal reluctantly sat. Mo promptly grabbed the hookah pipe, took a long draw on it, and exhaled slowly.

"I finally had the chance to stop in Lebanon, and I figured I'd look you up," Kamal explained. "So what have you been up to?"

Mo took another long drag, blew it out, and grinned. "What have I been up to? Not much. And that's the way I like it."

"No, I mean, what happened to you after the orphanage?"

"Oh, yeah, that." Mo sighed. "Don't remember a lot of it. I was working for the government. Inspecting stuff. Every year, they'd promise us more money, but never did it."

"Did you get fired?" Kamal asked.

"Oh, no, nothing like that." Mo took another long hit. "No, man, I just got tired of it all." After another long exhale, he added, "Corruption, double standards, unkept promises, inflation. There's no hope. What's the point of working so hard if you can't afford food? After everything, I realized I didn't need a whole lot. Not like I thought I did."

"So you quit?"

"Sort of," Mo said, laughing. "I took a leave of absence. Never went back."

"I see."

"So what have you been up to?" Mo asked.

"I've been traveling, doing business," Kamal replied. "I stay pretty busy."

"That sounds cool." Mo took another long drag on the hookah. "I don't like being busy any more."

"But don't you want to do something?"

Mo paused for a second, and then laughed. "I *am* doing something."

"No, I mean, is this . . ." Kamal made an odd face. "Never mind. Where's your bathroom?"

Mo just pointed. Kamal rose and walked through the dark hallway until he saw the bathroom through one of the doors that was ajar.

He opened the door, stepped inside, and was greeted with the sight of a young woman sitting naked in the bathtub, soaking in the water. Her clothes, of which there weren't much, were piled on the floor next to the tub.

"Hi," she said, not even bothering to cover herself from Kamal's view.

Kamal laughed. "I didn't have to go that bad." He retreated to the living room, where Mo stared at the wall blankly.

"Who is she?" Kamal asked, also beginning to smile.

"She's here for the, uh . . . charity," Mo said. "For some reason, I'm popular with the ladies."

"So, what you're saying is," Kamal said, "you've been spending every last coin on hookers and drug dealers?" He shook his head. And laughed.

"Why not?" Mo said, throwing his hands wide. "I'm living the good life, my friend. I'm at peace. Nobody bothers me here. I eat, I sleep, I smoke. I hang with my friends when I want. I don't have to punch a time clock." He laughed and pointed at Kamal. "I'm happy. How many people can say that?"

Kamal looked around. "You could find a better place than this."

"I probably could," Mo said. "But I don't need a nice place to enjoy myself."

Kamal shook his head. As much as he was glad Mo was inexplicably happy, the squalor he lived in reminded Kamal of the orphanage. A little too much.

"Maybe you don't," Kamal said, "but I've left that world behind."

Mo took another long draw on the pipe, smiled, and exhaled slowly. "And yet, here you are."

Kamal watched the clouds of smoke swirl around, and shook his head again. "No," he said to himself. "I deserve more than a life of cheap hookers and weed."

• • • •

"When's the last time you just talked to people in the market?" Mo pointed to one booth in particular. "See that woman there? Her husband left her. If she doesn't sell her trinkets, she doesn't eat. I give her some money sometimes when she needs it."

"What do you get in return?" Kamal asked.

"I get her to keep me warm for the night," Mo said with a laugh. "That's worth something."

"If you say so," Kamal chuckled.

"Hey!" A voice from behind them made Mo turn around.

"Oh, hey, Abdel. How's it going, man?"

Abdel, a middle-aged man in a tattered jacket, shook his head. "I need that money you owe me," he said flatly. "I got debts to pay, too."

"Oh, hey, sorry," Mo said sheepishly. "Can I maybe get it to you tomorrow?"

"That's what you said last week," Abdel sighed. "Do you have it or not?"

Before Mo could answer, Kamal interrupted. "How much does he owe you?"

"About one hundred," Adbel said, and Mo nodded.

"Here," Kamal said, pulling out his wallet. "I'll cover it."

"Serious?" Mo said with a surprised look. "You don't have to do that, man. I'm sure I could . . ."

"No, it's fine," Kamal said. "Don't worry about it." He turned to Abdel and handed him a crisp bill. "Here you go."

"I see you have very loyal friends," Abdel said with a grin as he took the money. "I respect that, Mo. Thank you again."

As Abdel left, Mo turned to Kamal, his smile wide. "Thank you. Hey, since you're here, we should go get something to smoke!"

"If that's what you want," Kamal answered. "Where to?"

Mo turned and led Kamal through a series of turns, side streets, and makeshift booths. A few minutes later, they had found a back alley, lined with boxes, with a steel door at the end.

Mo knocked on the door and waited.

"Who's there?"

"It's me, Mohammed."

"What do you want?"

"I wanna buy some hash."

The door clanked, and then creaked open. A tall, thin man in a turban stood there, glaring. "Who's your friend here?"

"Ah, he's good," Mo said. "You got anything fresh?"

The man shook his head. "You still owe me from a month ago!"

"No way! How much?" Mo asked. He tried to crunch numbers in his head and failed after a few seconds.

"I want a thousand, or you can go somewhere else."

"Do I have that much on my tab?" Mo frowned.

"This isn't a bar," the thin man said. "You don't have a tab. You pay what you owe us, or we'll come take it from you."

Kamal cleared his throat. "I'll cover his debt. If I give you one thousand, he's good?"

Mo just stood there,

"Yes, that will do," the man said. Kamal once again pulled out his billfold and peeled off bills until the man smiled. "That enough?" Kamal asked.

"Yes, thank you very much." The man ducked out of view for a moment, and reappeared with a small paper package, about the size of his fist. "Here you go"

The metal door slammed shut with a clang.

"Hey, Kamal, you didn't have to do that." Mo's face briefly showed some emotion. "You know I can't repay you."

"I know," Kamal said. "But I have the satisfaction of knowing your debts are settled. If it's one thing I can't stand," he added, "it's unpaid debts."

As Kamal turned to leave, he thought of Al-Fahad. It was very likely that Al-Fahad's men were looking for him at that exact moment. Suddenly, a thought crossed his mind.

"Mo, can I ask you something?"

"Sure," Mo said. "Anything."

"Can I crash at your place for a few days?"

• • • •

For the next three days, Kamal lived like Mo lived. They ate fast food in the market, they listened to live bands playing at the nearby clubs, and they smoked as much hash and weed as Kamal could find. Everything became a blur, and Kamal started to wonder if time was passing at all.

At one point, Kamal remembered the girl that he had stumbled upon in Mo's bathroom. That night, they went down a few blocks to the tourist area, and spotted a handful of girls in miniskirts hanging around on the street corner. None of them were very pretty, but they weren't exactly repulsive.

Kamal figured if this were to be his last few nights on earth, he might as well enjoy himself.

The next thing Kamal remembered was waking up naked in Mo's living room. The air was thick with smoke and haze, but he could make out piles of empty beer cans, half-eaten food, and ashtrays full of cigarette butts and leftover joints. There was a mirror and a small bag of cocaine on the table. Three hookers, still in their underwear, were passed out on a dirty mattress in the corner. Mo was curled up on the sofa, sleeping like the dead, and snoring loudly.

As he stood, Kamal's head threatened to split open. He steadied himself, and when the room stopped spinning, he managed to find his pants and wallet. He threw them on, and made his way to the door through the piles of bottles and clothes.

He opened the front door, turned, and took one last look at Mo. It was both heartwarming and saddening to see his old friend again. Kamal was glad their paths had crossed, but he knew it would be the last time they would see each other.

He stepped out into the sunlight, closed the door behind him, and didn't look back again.

• • • •

It was late when Kamal finally arrived at the casino where it had all started. The exterior hadn't changed at all in the years he'd worked for Al-Fahad. He parked the car, crossed the street, and took a deep breath. The door had a red and white *closed* sign hanging on it. With a calm expression, he swung the door open and stepped inside.

Inside, the lights were on, but nobody was gaming inside. The rows of slot machines were dark and silent.

At the back of the casino, flanked by two guards, was the door to Al-Fahad's office. Kamal approached, and with a nod, opened the door and walked in.

"There you are, Kamal." Al-Fahad was seated behind a desk, holding a cigar in one hand and a glass of brandy in the other. "I was expecting you sooner."

Kamal just nodded. He closed the door behind him, approached the desk and stopped, and put his hands in his pockets.

"I suppose you think you're clever?" Al-Fahad smiled and exhaled a puff of cigar smoke. "And I'd agree with you. In fact, you're one of the most resourceful men I've ever met. But there are times when even the best men make mistakes. I am willing to forgive. Which is more than you'd get from most."

Kamal tilted his head, but said nothing. His eyes glared.

Al-Fahad gave a low chuckle. "Do you know why you have that look in your eye?"

Kamal blinked. "What?"

"That look, those eyes. When you're about to kill someone. You got that look from me." Al-Fahad leaned back in his chair. "I know you want to kill me, because of what happened in Egypt, and threatening the girl. But. . ."

He leaned in closer and smiled. "You wouldn't kill your own father, would you?"

"You've gone crazy old man. I think you are starting to lose your mind." Kamal started laughing

In a flash, Kamal pulled a knife from his jacket and lunged towards Al-Fahad, but as he raised his hand, there was a loud pop.

Kamal looked down, realizing that he had just been shot in the leg. He dropped to one knee as the knife clattered to the floor. He grabbed where the bullet had struck, and his entire world burst into pain. Blood flowed freely through his hand, down his leg, and onto the floor.

"You bastard!" Kamal snarled through clenched teeth. "I'll kill you for that!"

"Technically, you're the bastard." Al-Fahad chuckled, but kept the gun pointed at Kamal.

"I've been watching you since you were a little boy, after she dropped you off at the orphanage. I saw it all. When your friend died- when the girl was raped- when the manager died- when you were robbing tourists at the resort. The scams, the hustles. I know everything. I have eyes and ears everywhere."

Kamal's head was spinning. How could Al-Fahad have known those things? Could it be possible that he was telling the truth? He struggled to think of what to say, but nothing made sense.

"Do you think our meeting at this casino was an accident?" He let out a hearty laugh. "My boy, there is nothing to say. Kamal, I know I've left you out there, alone. It was because I wanted you to be strong, not like your step brothers. Spoiled little brats that can't even kill a fly."

Al-Fahad laughed again. "No, I wanted a heartless son to come and rule this organization with me, to do my bidding with loyalty and precision. To not ask questions."

"What makes you think I care about you or your organization?" Kamal's hands clenched into fists. "I'm not like you. I don't need anybody's help . . ."

Al-Fahad's face went serious. "Enough with excuses. Kamal, your entire life was part of my plan. In fact," he leaned in closer. "You wouldn't be the man you are today if it weren't for me." Al-Fahad straightened himself and walked back behind his desk. "You owe me your life."

"I don't owe you shit!" Kamal spat. His head was starting to get light from the loss of blood, but he refused to show it.

"I want you to know that I would have never harmed the girl. I was testing your loyalty towards those you love." Al-Fahad put the gun back in his jacket holster, and smiled. "If you would have let someone threaten her without wanting to kill him, I would have been disappointed."

"I'm still considering it." Kamal was struggling to hold himself together.

"It's true that you are angry, and you need time to think and digest everything I've said. But I know one day, you will be back asking for my help." Al-Fahad raised a finger and pointed at Kamal. "You can run, boy, but you will always be in my shadow. I know this, because at the end of the day, everyone needs an Al-Fahd in their life. And every son needs his father."

Kamal shook his head. "I don't think so, old man. I don't need anybody!" He slowly got to his feet, making sure not to put weight on his bad leg. Despite the waves of pain, Kamal locked eyes with the man claiming to be his father. His expression was dead serious. "Are you done lecturing me?" Without waiting for an answer, he turned and headed for the door.

"You may go, Kamal. But before you leave, I want to tell you one last thing."

Kamal stopped, but didn't turn around. "What is it?" he hissed.

"My real name is Hakeem."

Without glancing back, Kamal straightened his jacket and walked to the office door. He twisted the knob, opened it, and stepped through into the casino's main floor.

All of this had been a waste of time. Kamal wasn't going to get his revenge. Or could he?

Kamal looked at the two guards there, and an idea came to his mind.

Lightning fast, Kamal grabbed the gun from the first guard's hip and pulled the trigger three times. The guard staggered back and crumpled to the ground, shocked. Before the second guard could react, Kamal swung the gun under his arm and shot the second guard in the chest twice.

"What's going on?!"

Kamal strode back through the door into Al-Fahad's office and leveled the guard's pistol right at Al-Fahad.

"You can't do this to me!"

One trigger pull. Then two. Then three.

Kamal kept pulling the trigger until the gun was empty. He couldn't tell how many times he'd hit Al-Fahad, but between the blood loss and the ringing in his ears, he could barely stand. Everything turned red.

And just like that, Kamal realized what he had done. He threw the empty gun down and headed for the main entrance. His heart still pounding, his mind racing.

He hobbled through the door, across the street, and jumped into his car. In seconds, he was pulling into the street. With a roar and a screech, Kamal fled as fast as his car could go. His heart raced uncontrollably. His hands tingled, his entire body still shaking from the adrenaline. In return for his freedom, he was now a marked man.

• • • •.

The first thing Kamal saw when he stepped out of the airport in Crete was a row of taxis, and a pay phone booth. He looked around and stepped inside.

He dropped in a few coins, picked up the receiver, and punched in a number.

"Hello, this is Mr. Ledet. I'm calling about the house I listed for sale last week."

"Bonjour! Good to hear from you. What can we help you with?" the voice on the other end said.

"I would like to lower the price by at least one hundred thousand. I want it to sell as quickly as possible."

"Are you sure? That would cut out most of your profit on the contract."

"I'm sure," Kamal affirmed. "I just need it sold. You can throw the car in as well."

"Yes sir, we will handle that for you."

As Kamal wrapped up the call and hung up the phone, he heard a car horn beep.

He stepped out of the booth and smiled. Nicolette was there, sitting in a bright yellow convertible, wearing a matching sunflower dress and dark sunglasses.

Hopping into the car, Kamal laughed and shook his head. "I thought I told you to blend in?"

Nicolette slid her shades down her nose. "This is Crete. I *am* blending in."

She revved the car's motor and pulled away from the curb. Once they had cleared the parking lot, she shot Kamal a glance. "So how did your trip to Lebanon go?"

"I've got some bad news."

Nicolette, not sure what to say, just nodded.

"I don't know where to begin." Kamal sighed and closed his eyes. "I went to meet with Al-Fahad. He told me some wild story to manipulate me, and we ended up shooting each other. I killed two of his guards as well."

It took a moment for the statement to sink in.

"What . . . What do you mean? You killed him? He *shot* you?"

Kamal's expression darkened. "We're not going to be able to go back to the house in France. It's not safe there for us any more."

"So." Nicolette slowly shook her head. "That's what this was all about then? How did this happen?"

"I thought I was going there to get even, but things didn't work out that way," Kamal said sharply. "Al-Fahad was trying to ruin my life. This was our only option." He paused, let out a deep sigh, and added quietly, "We need to get as far away from here as possible."

Nicolette's eyes narrowed. "So what's the plan now?"

"The plan all along," Kamal said, "was to have enough money to live how we want to live."

"And? Then what?"

"And then that's exactly what we're going to do."

CHAPTER 12

PART I
VENGEANCE

"**K**amal, I think someone's following us."

Kamal glanced in the rearview mirror. Sure enough, a black Mercedes was pacing them, turn-for-turn, about four cars back.

"Keep going." Kamal nodded. "It might be Al-Fahad's men. Or one of his friends. You know where the main market is?"

"Of course." She pressed the accelerator, and the little convertible smoothed forward into a gap in traffic.

About six minutes later, Nicolette pulled into an empty parking spot on the busy street and shut the car off. Kamal jumped out without opening the door as Nicolette walked around.

Kamal nodded. "Follow me." The courtyard was filled with people coming and going, mostly shoppers and tourists. They eventually came across a small cafe, went inside, and approached the counter. A young waitress smiled and took their order. Kamal paid her upfront.

"We're going to have to go somewhere Al-Fahad hasn't done business," Kamal stated.

Nicolette nodded. "What about Spain?"

"Possibly. I was thinking further . . . north. Maybe England."

"Here you go." The girl behind the counter handed Kamal a paper bag with falafels.

As Kamal thanked her, shouting outside snapped him to attention.

"Time for us to go?" Nicolette asked, snarfing a bite.

"Absolutely. Go out the back."

Nicolette nodded and wiped her mouth with a napkin. "I'll go first."

As Nicolette exited, Kamal scanned the crowd through the window. After a few seconds, he walked to the rear of the bistro, into the kitchen, and strode through to the rear exit without stopping. He emerged into the alleyway and immediately knew they were in a bad situation.

Nicolette was crouching behind a dumpster. To the right, Kamal could hear more shouting. Someone was making their way down the alley.

Kamal pulled Nicolette along as he bolted through the next open door. In one smooth motion, he swung her ahead of him, spun around, and locked the door behind him.

"That way." He grunted.

As they popped out of the kitchen into the neighboring diner, Kamal snagged a hat from a customer's head, put it on, and calmly walked out the front door. He made a beeline through the crowd into a shop opposite of it.

They walked into the souvenir shop and approached the counter in the back. A portly man with an equally round mustache smiled at them.

"How may I help you?"

"Excuse me. Is there a bathroom back there?" Nicolette said in an upbeat tone.

"Yes, certainly," he replied, looking her up and down.

Nicolette gave him a little nod, then walked through the hallway and an open back door, into another wide street.

"Okay, now what?"

Looking around, Kamal spotted an old motorized scooter leaning against a lamppost. "There," he said, pointing. "Let's go."

He took a quick look at the scooter and determined it was rideable, despite its rough appearance. After flipping the fuel valve on, Kamal quickly found the ignition switch, yanked two wires from it, and twisted them together. He then swung his leg over the seat and stomped on the kickstart, which caused the scooter to sputter and crackle to life.

Nicolette smiled and shook her head "OK, let's go."

With a blip of the throttle, they pulled away from the curb and buzzed down the street, towards the coast, away from the center of town.

• • • •

"We've been on this boat for three hours," Nicolette said, somewhat impatiently. "When are we going to get there?"

Kamal stood at the helm, watching for signs of anything suspicious. So far, they had managed to slide past everyone unnoticed. Crete, and the rest of Greece, were far behind them. The forty-foot boat slid through the waves with ease.

"I think another hour and we'll be at a stopping point." Kamal turned and gave her a little smile. "We'll have to get fuel and something to eat, but we'll be on the mainland before dawn. From there, we can take a plane back to France."

"Do you mind if I close my eyes for a few minutes?"

Kamal shook his head. "That's fine. I'll wake you up." As Nicolette went down the stairs into the cabin below, Kamal rubbed his eyes to clear his head. He wasn't sure how long they could remain incognito, but the countryside was large enough that it was possible.

As the evening city lights slid past into darkness, the radio crackled and hissed intermittently. Nothing came through except background noise. Kamal had a hunch there would be people on the lookout for them, but as long as they didn't bring attention to themselves, they could live in peace. He hoped.

The rest of the boat ride was uneventful, which Kamal was thankful for. After having bounced through Tinos and Gavrio, he eventually spotted the harbor in Rafina, on the east side of Athens.

Finding a place to anchor the boat wasn't too difficult, but Kamal wasn't worried about returning for it, either. They would need to find a way to get to an airport that had private planes for hire, and take a chartered plane up the coast. All the major airports would probably be under surveillance, and Kamal didn't want to leave any traces of where he'd been.

Kamal took the stairs down into the cabin, where Nicolette was just waking up.

"Where are we?" she asked in a sleepy voice.

"We just pulled into Athens." He smiled. "Grab your bag. We're going to catch a plane."

Nicolette just nodded, then gathered her things. Kamal watched her for a few seconds, just admiring her dedication and beauty. He left the cabin and headed back on deck where he began tying off the boat to the pier.

The airport in Elliniko, just south of Athens, was only a few miles away from the coast. They were able to catch a cab, though it was close to midnight. By the time they got onto the airport grounds, it was almost dawn.

At the counter, Kamal went to work booking a private flight to leave that morning, as soon as they had someone available. They managed to grab a small plane that was headed to Italy, with the hopes to find another one returning to France once they were there.

As they boarded the plane, Kamal took a look around the Greek countryside. It was a nice place, maybe even someplace he'd like to live, but it would have to wait.

"I hear they're going to open the tunnel soon," Nicolette said, glancing up from her seat.

"It would make going back and forth so much easier," Kamal said, taking the seat next to her. "I hate taking ferries to London. They're too slow."

"Kamal?" Nicolette pulled her ever-present sunglasses down and looked Kamal in the eyes.

"Yes, Nicolette?"

"Do you have a plan?"

Kamal narrowed his eyes.

"I *always* have a plan."

• • • •

Before Kamal realized it, the days had turned to weeks, which turned into months. Twelve months, in fact, had passed since they had fled from Greece to England. It had taken almost a year for Kamal to not constantly be on edge, but he was eventually getting used to it.

They'd found a nice flat to buy on the outskirts of London. Nothing conspicuous, but still in a nice neighborhood. They were within proximity of everything they needed. Life had finally become peaceful for them. This morning in particular, however, was different from all the others.

Just before sunrise, Kamal got dressed and packed a small bag with supplies he'd need. He was dressed in traveling clothes, not business attire.

Daylight was breaking as Kamal pulled his car, a TVR S1, out of the parking spot and onto the street. The engine purred as he sped east, out of town, towards the coast. The Folkestone rail station that utilized the new Channel Tunnel had just opened, and Kamal was looking forward to the opportunity to use it.

Close to an hour later, Kamal pulled into the station and parked. The train was scheduled to leave within the hour, and promised a short trip directly into Paris.

As Kamal boarded the train, he looked back across the city and thought of Nicolette, probably just now waking up and reading his note. He knew she wouldn't understand, but it was the only thing he'd been thinking of the entire year they'd been there.

Kamal told himself it would be a short trip. But business trips rarely are. Especially when there is unfinished business.

• • • •

"I SWEAR! I didn't do anything!"

The room was dimly lit, but there was enough light for Joseph to make out Kamal's face. He pulled fiercely on his bonds, but despite his youthful strength, the ropes wouldn't budge.

"Your father was a good, but naive man." Kamal leaned in closer.

"He just wanted to sell paintings. He wasn't trying to ruin anybody!"

"None of that matters now." Kamal snapped.

"You ruined our family!" Joseph shouted. "My father killed himself because of what happened!"

"At least he died by his own hand," Kamal replied.

"Why are you doing this to me?!" Joseph pleaded. "You got what you wanted. Right?"

"Oh, yes," Kamal said. "But you almost took something from me, and that is inexcusable."

Joseph's jaw dropped. "The girl?! Is this about the girl?!"

"There's nothing you can say to make things better." He casually pulled a knife from his bag and held it up in front of Joseph's face. "Nobody hurts the one person I love."

"Please stop!" Joseph begged. "I'll give you anything you want! This doesn't have to be hard! I've still got some money left over, you can have whatever's left . . ."

Kamal nodded. "I'll get what I want." He slowly dragged the knife across Joseph's face, leaving behind a growing crimson line that flowed down to his mouth.

In a flash of movement, Kamal drew the knife around and plunged it into Joseph's shoulder, eliciting a scream. Blood began flowing freely down his arm. Kamal's ears rang from Joseph's screams. He stood and stepped back.

Joseph's head flopped to the side as he slid in and out of consciousness. Within minutes, the entire floor was covered in blood.

"How does it feel?" Kamal sneered. "Do you like the way that blade feels?"

Joseph, somehow knowing it would be over soon, managed to pull his head up. With every ounce of strength he could muster, he spit a mouthful of blood at Kamal.

"Animal . . . you're . . . an animal."

Kamal tilted his head and leaned in close again, until his lips were touching Joseph's ear.

"I'm the angel of pain," he whispered.

With a shout, Kamal plunged the knife upwards, into Joseph's jaw, through soft palate, into his brain.

Kamal stood. He kicked Joseph's now lifeless body in the chest, causing it to fall over backwards still tied to the chair, and hit the floor with a sickening thud.

"Now," Kamal panted, "one more debt to settle."

• • • •

"Where are we going?" Nicolette smiled and gave Kamal a playful look.

"You saw the boarding passes. We're going to Switzerland."

"I know that," she replied. "But why?"

"I've got a special job for you." Kamal said. "How do you feel about ski resorts?"

"Seriously?" Nicolette grinned widely. "It sounds like fun!"

"I'm going to need you to take this one seriously," Kamal said. "There's a lot at stake."

"Of course," Nicolette said. "I've missed our adventures. Who's the target this time?"

"His name," he said, handing her a folder, "is Rafael."

Nicolette flipped the folder open and glanced through it. "You've done your research as usual. This guy looks young—he should be pretty easy to convince."

"He's currently studying in London, but he's also working remotely for his father's business."

"So what's the plan?"

"When we land in Switzerland, you're going to sign up for off-season ski lessons. We're going to see to it that Rafael here meets you."

"Pretty standard routine then?"

"Not exactly," Kamal said. "I'm interested in making contact with his father."

"Ah, business stuff, right." Nicolette sat back in her seat and sighed. "I guess I'll just do what I'm good at."

"And what is that?"

Nicolette smiled. "Ripping hearts out."

• • • •

"Do you mind if I ride with you?" Nicolette stood next to the ski lift, smiling. She was wearing a brightly colored ski jacket and holding a pair of skis in one hand, and poles in the other.

Rafael smiled. "No, of course I don't mind."

As the next lift came around, they both hopped on and began their ascent. Nicolette took a long look at him. Rafael was tall, with a square jaw framed by dark curls. His blue eyes were clear, and his shoulders were broad. She caught herself staring, but played it off with a shy smile. His smile was infectious.

"Hi, I'm Suzette." "Nice to meet you."

"I'm Rafael. I haven't seen you around. Are you new at skiing?"

"Sort of. I usually ski in France, that's where I'm from." She smiled again. The lift was now gliding upwards over huge sweeping swatches of pristine white snow.

"I love the view from the lift," Rafael said. "It's like we're birds, flying over the mountain."

"I do love the mountains. But what about you? Where are you from?"

"Ah, yes." Rafael shrugged. "My family is from Lebanon, but I live in London right now. I'm working as a manager for my father's business, and taking classes at night." He let out a deep sigh. "But I decided to come out here to get away from all that. I really love the outdoors, especially the mountains."

"You sound very busy! What does your company do?"

"A little bit of everything. Mostly trading goods, investing, things like that." He looked at Nicolette's outfit and nodded. "You must work somewhere, too. What do you do when you're not skiing?"

Nicolette smirked and looked away. "I've been all over. Mostly working with businesses, art appraisal, lots of other things."

"No kidding!" Rafael let out a low whistle. "You're quite the surprise!"

"Why is that surprising?"

"Well. . ." He stammered for a bit, then grinned. "Seeing a beautiful woman like you, I just assumed you were just someone's girlfriend." He gave a nod. "I'm sorry I thought that of you. My apologies."

Nicolette raised an eyebrow. "It's been years since I've met someone that honest."

Rafael blushed, giving her a sheepish smile. "I wasn't raised in the best home. I decided as a young man that I wasn't going to be anything like my father."

Nicolette found her cheeks were flushing a bit involuntarily. But before she could say anything, the lift reached the top of the slope, and they were forced to dismount.

"I hope to see you again," Rafael said with a smile. "Be careful out there."

As he pulled his goggles down and began moving towards the beginning of the run, Nicolette caught herself staring.

No, she thought to herself. *This is strictly business.*

But Rafael's words played back in her mind, over and over. Was she really just someone's girl? How many years had she been letting Kamal determine her fate?

Angrily, she shook the thoughts from her head—that kind of thinking was unproductive. Kamal had always been there for her, and had never asked for anything in return. He had even saved her life, more than once.

But no matter what she told herself, the seed had been planted.

• • • •

When Kamal and Nicolette visited the ski resort again in January, a month had passed. The slopes were fresh and smooth from the previous week's snowfall, and throngs of people were enjoying the resort.

As they stepped off the shuttle, Nicolette breathed in the crisp coolness. The scent of evergreens and the burble of people's chatter filled the air.

Kamal picked up his bag and scanned the crowd. "Let's go get a cabin before all the nice ones are taken." They entered the main lodge, and approached the front desk. The room was enormous, with rough wooden beams above and large fur rugs below.

After checking in, they made their way around the resort until they reached a row of small log cabins strung along the side of the mountain, each with its own stockpile of cordwood stacked in front. Kamal looked at his key, counted the cabins, and pointed. "This one."

Kamal opened the door, and Nicolette walked in, immediately flopping down on the small couch. "What a shuttle ride," she sighed.

Kamal dropped his suitcase next to the door and nodded. "You'd think they would get buses that aren't fifty years old."

Nicolette looked up at Kamal, and gave him a curious look.

"Are you going skiing, Kamal? I mean, since we're here. . ."

"I have things to attend to," he said flatly. "You're welcome to hit the slopes. Just make sure. . ."

"Yeah, I know," she interrupted. "I know what to do."

"This is important," Kamal insisted. "I wouldn't have brought you here if it wasn't."

Nicolette replied by closing her eyes. Eventually, Kamal finished unpacking his things and left, presumably to go look around.

Nicolette sat up and sighed. Pulling her suitcase onto the sofa next to her, she began pulling out an outfit consisting of a cute parka, some form-fitting insulated pants, and a colorful wool hat. She took the clothes into the bathroom, changed, and left the cabin, locking the door behind her.

It wasn't long before she found the main slope lift, and settled in to watch people. There were families there with children, young people, old people, and what seemed like every kind of accent imaginable. It was vivid and full of energy, like the beach, but without the noise of the ocean and seagulls.

Nicolette looked around for a minute before she realized she was a little nervous. Was it excitement over seeing Rafael again? No, it was probably just nerves.

"Excuse me, Suzette?"

Nicolette snapped her head around. Standing behind her, in a forest green vest, was Rafael.

"Oh!" she exclaimed. "I didn't see you there!" Her face broke into a smile.

"It's good to see you again. Are you here on vacation?"

"Um . . ."

Rafael laughed and shook his head. "I'm sorry. That was a dumb question." He paused for a second, then smiled. "I'm not ready to ski yet, so would you like to go get something to eat with me?" His eyes locked with hers, unwavering.

Nicolette nodded. "Absolutely"

Inside the main lodge, they found a small dining area with wooden tables that had tops made out of huge cross-sections of tree trunks. They sat down and looked at the menus.

"What kind of food do you like?" Rafael asked. "There's not a huge selection here."

"I'm not too picky," Nicolette replied, "as long as it's fresh and hot. Where I come from, the food is incomparable, so I try not to set my expectations too high."

"Why would you settle for low expectations?" Rafael said with a wry grin. "What kind of expectations *should* you have?"

Nicolette, caught somewhat off guard, laughed nervously. "I suppose that's true of most of my life, really." She looked into Rafael's intense gaze, and something in her mind urged her to tell him the truth.

"I was raised in a good environment," she said softly. "My family loved me, more than anything. I was an only child."

Rafael raised an eyebrow.

Nicolette, suddenly flooded with memories, bit her lip until her voice steadied again. "My parents were both killed in a car accident when I was a girl. I moved to France with an aunt. She raised me. No one but her expected me to amount to anything. She is . . . she passed away. Recently."

"I'm so sorry to hear that!" Rafael reached over and placed his hand on hers, giving it a light squeeze. "I'm sure that must have been difficult."

"I don't know why I'm telling you this," she said with a chuckle. "Now that you know a bit more about me, what was your childhood like?"

"My father is a businessman, so I didn't see him very much. Every now and then, he'd take trips to the city and bring me and my mother with him, but we did our own thing. My mother was an amazing woman." Rafael smiled. "She set my standards pretty high."

"I suppose we should look at the menu," Nicolette said as her stomach growled. "I didn't realize how hungry I was!"

They placed their order, and then proceeded to talk for another hour while the tourists milled about all around them. Every question she asked was answered directly, and more than once, Nicolette caught herself before she said something too personal. His demeanor was very disarming, and conversation flowed effortlessly. By the time they had finished eating and the table had been cleared, the sun had started to set.

Rafael stood and held out his hand. "Suzette, would you be so kind as to take a walk with me?"

Nicolette glanced up at the clock on the wall, and winced. "It's getting late. I should probably get some sleep if I'm going to do any skiing tomorrow."

"Very well," Rafael said. "At least let me walk you to your cabin. That's the very least I can do after the wonderful time we've had." He extended his hand, and after a second, Nicolette took it.

As they left the main lodge, the first glimpses of twilight had started to appear, and a few bright stars twinkled here and there. Nicolette looked up into the sky, and felt something stir deep inside. It was serene and beautiful. Powerful, and yet peaceful.

While she was looking up, Nicolette's foot slid on a patch of ice, and she suddenly found herself slamming into the frozen ground, rather hard.

"Oh my god! Are you OK?" Rafael knelt down and wrapped his arm around her shoulder. "Are you hurt?"

Nicolette tried to put her feet under her, grimaced, then sat back down again. "I think I rolled my ankle. Hurts pretty bad."

"Damn!" Rafael shook his head. "I should have been paying more attention. I wasn't looking at the ground."

"I think I'll be OK," Nicolette said. "It's not broken. But I don't think I'll be able to walk on it for a couple of days."

Rafael gave her a discouraging look. "Well, come on, I'll help you up. No use sitting out here in the cold." He bent down, wrapped one arm around her torso, and put his other hand under her knees "Ready? On the count of three."

Nicolette nodded. "One, two, three!" Carefully, Rafael stood and cradled her in his arms. She wrapped her free arm around his neck to steady herself.

"OK," he said, "Let's take it slow. Which way is your cabin?"

Nicolette pointed, and Rafael began down the walkway to where the path turned and split off, leading to the first row of cabins. Rafael carried her until they were at the doorway. He carefully swung her upright, making sure she had her balance.

Nicolette pulled out her key and opened the door, revealing a cozy little living room with the fireplace already supplied with wood and burning happily. Holding on to the wall, she managed to make her way around to the sofa, and gently lower herself onto it, making sure to swing her foot up on the cushions to keep it elevated.

"How's that?" Rafael asked with some concern. "Do you need help getting your boots off?"

Nicolette thought for a second, then nodded. "I think so. I can feel it swelling."

Rafael closed the door behind him, shutting out the frigid night air. He quickly went to work, sitting across from Nicolette, and began working her boot off of the afflicted foot. She tried not to protest too much, but it was definitely twisted. Eventually, he succeeded in removing her boot and sock, and began gently probing the swollen area.

"Ow! That hurts!" she blurted. "Can you be a little more gentle?"

Rafael smiled. "All you had to do was ask." He began slowly caressing her foot, rubbing his fingers all around the ankle, making sure to move slowly.

And then, just like that, Rafael pulled away with a confused look on his face.

"Suzette, I don't know if this is really appropriate. . ."

She sat up and tried to look into his eyes, but saw he was avoiding eye contact.

"What's the matter?"

"I've really enjoyed our evening," he began. "But it would be inappropriate for me to be here alone with you."

"Are you worried about what people think?"

"No," he replied. "I'm worried about what *you* think."

Nicolette felt that tug again, but ignored it.

"Rafael, you're one of the most honest people I know." She reached out and grabbed his hand firmly.

Slowly, and with some effort, Nicolette managed to stand up holding on to both the sofa and Rafael's arm. She pulled herself up as high as she could and wrapped her arms around his neck, pulling him in close.

"I could really fall for a man like you," she whispered, her breath hot as she leaned in to kiss him. For once, she almost believed it.

But instead, her lips touched his hand that he had put between them. Surprised, she just looked at him.

"I'm sorry," he said softly, his fingers still touching her lips. "But I need to let you rest."

Nicolette just stood there, dumbfounded. Her heart was still racing, but she suddenly realized that her foot was not happy with being upright. She let out a little gasp and plopped back onto the sofa unceremoniously, causing Rafael to break out into laughter.

"You'd better take care of that," he said. "It doesn't look like you'll be walking on it just yet."

Nicolette just blushed and nodded. "Yeah, I'll ice it in a minute."

Silence hung in the air for a few seconds, until Rafael snapped to attention.

"Here," he said, holding his hand out. "My phone number is on this business card. Feel free to drop me a message whenever you like." He gave a half-smile, and added, "I'd really like that."

And just like that, Rafael opened the door and disappeared into the cold, leaving Nicolette determined to take him up on the offer.

• • • •

Kamal walked through the fresh snow, trying to be careful as he made his way towards the ski lodge. In the distance, Kamal could see people bustling about, enjoying themselves.

He paused for a second and listened. He'd heard something that caught his ear.

It was laughter. But not just any laughter—it was Nicolette's voice. Kamal knew it well.

He rounded the bend in the path, and as he looked, he saw Nicolette, her arm wrapped around Rafael, laughing and smiling. She was beaming, like a springtime flower in bloom.

Rafael leaned in to whisper something in her ear, and their lips met.

Something deep inside of Kamal stirred. The rush of emotions came quickly, and he closed his eyes for a moment as waves of anger washed over him.

Why was he angry? Nicolette was doing exactly what she was supposed to. Rafael was eating out of her hand.

And then Kamal realized the truth—Nicolette looked *happy*. And the man she was with wasn't him. All the years Kamal had looked after her, and she had found happiness with someone else.

At that moment, Kamal knew there would be nothing that could stop him from exacting revenge,

It would be more sweet than justice could ever be.

• • • •

Springtime in London was only distinguished from winter by the color of the haze, but there was still enough sunlight to make being outside comfortable.

Nicolette sat at a small patio table, enjoying every bit of sun she could get. The winter had been long, and she was ready to get back to enjoying the beach and feeling the warmth on her skin.

A moment later, Rafael appeared, holding a tray with fish and chips. He carefully arranged the food and sat down, flashing Nicolette a bright smile.

"Raphael, do you remember the story I told you about growing up with my aunt in France?"

"I think so," he said. "Why?"

"What was your childhood like?" Nicolette's eyes honed in on his. "How did you end up being the man you are when you were raised in . . ."

"I'm nothing like my father," he said quietly. "I appreciate that he's given us nice things, but he can be a very cruel man." He thought for a second, then added, "I really never felt loved by him. But I suppose my mother more than made up for that."

"She must have loved you very much."

"She did. But what about your story?" Raphael reached out and gently touched her hand. "How does someone as beautiful as you not end up completely twisted by the world?"

"Well," she sighed, "that's not entirely true. I wasn't raised in Paris." Her smile faded. "In fact, after my parents died in that car wreck, I ended up living with my mother's parents in Lebanon."

Raphael nodded.

"I was an illegitimate child, and my parents loved me and kept me, even though it was against their religion. But my grandmother didn't agree. I can remember . . ." Her voice choked up a bit, but she swallowed and continued.

"I can remember begging her to let me stay there with them. I was fourteen. My grandfather wanted me, he fought for me. But in the end, her religion won out." She sniffled. Her eyes looked distant. "I remember them dropping me off at the orphanage. I screamed and cried for them to let me go. They pulled me out of my grandfather's arms, and I never saw them again."

Stunned, Raphael just shook his head. For a while, he just let the heaviness sit in the air.

"I'm so sorry," he whispered. "That must have been horrible."

Nicolette forced a smile. "I survived it. I learned how to fight. I decided to move forward with my life." She wiped her eyes and laughed. "With help, of course." And just like that, her impenetrable face returned. She couldn't believe she had opened up to him like that, but

Raphael's face softened a bit. "I have a favor to ask of you, Suzette, my love." Rafael held her hands and drew her closer.

"I'm sure it will be something interesting," she replied. "You're not one to disappoint."

"I would like," he said, swallowing hard, "to take you back home with me."

"Oh!" she said, feigning shock. "You're so bold!"

"Ha!" Rafael grinned. "No, I mean I'm going back home to visit my family soon, and I'd like for you to come with me to meet them."

"Oh, I see." She thought for a second. "We've been seeing each other for a few months now, right?"

Rafael nodded as he chewed.

"I think that's enough time to know whether I will offend your parents or not."

He let out a little snort. "I'm not concerned with you offending them. I just think it's appropriate."

"I think you're right," Nicolette said. "When would we be going, then?"

"You have to agree to go first," he teased.

"Fine." She rolled her eyes. "I'll agree to go meet your parents."

"Excellent!" he said, clapping his hands together. "Can you be ready to go this weekend?"

Raising an eyebrow, she shot him a disapproving look. "That's kind of short notice."

"I know you don't have anything scheduled," he said. "You told me so yourself."

"That's true."

"So what do you say? Can you be ready to leave by Friday?"

"I think so," she replied. "I'll need to let. . . my landlord knows I'll be gone for a while."

• • • •

"Welcome to our estate." Rafael waved his hand, as Nicolette just took it all in.

In the years she had traveled across Europe, she had stayed in some incredible houses. But this one was bigger than anything she'd been in— even bigger than the villa in France. The gardens spread across acres of rolling hills and paths, dotted with fruit trees and rows of vineyard grapes. The house itself dwarfed the hill it was on, to where it looked almost out of place. Everything had been freshly cleaned, swept, and trimmed. It was like a painting on a postcard.

"This is amazing!" Nicolette gushed. "What a beautiful garden!"

"I knew you'd like it," Rafael beamed. "I had them tidy everything up for your arrival. Couldn't not have it looking its best when you would be here to see it."

They walked through the courtyard, around the driveway, and up the main stairway into the front entrance. Nicolette's flowing floral print gown echoed the beautiful greenery along the way.

When they got to the entrance, the door swung open, and standing there was Rafael's father. When she saw his face, Nicolette's blood turned cold.

It was the same Mr. Farouk that had raped her at the orphanage, all those years ago.

It was why Kamal had wanted her to meet Rafael in the first place. It wasn't just about the money. But even so, knowing what she knew, seeing him made her flesh crawl.

"Father, I want you to meet Suzette!" Rafael put his arm around her shoulders, smiling ear to ear.

"Welcome to our household! I'm afraid your mother is away running errands, but she will return momentarily." He turned to Nicolette, his eyes boring into her very being. "You are quite a beautiful young woman! I can see why Rafael likes you." His stare lingered.

Nicolette maintained her bright smile, but inside, she was looking for any clues that Mr. Farouk might have recognized her. If he did, he showed no signs.

"Come, come inside!" he said, motioning them through the door. "We have dinner prepared. Everything is ready, and your mother will be here any minute."

Inside the mansion, there were golden mirrors, candelabras, and gilded pottery everywhere. It was like a museum, but without the velvet ropes. The trio made their way into the dining hall, where a table had been lavishly prepared with every kind of dish.

"This is traditional Lebanese cuisine," Rafael said. "I hope you like it!"

"I have high expectations," she replied with a wink.

"If you will excuse me for a moment," Rafael said with a slight bow, "I'd like to go wash up. Please excuse me!"

As he exited, Nicolette sat alone with Mr. Farouk, who was staring intently at her.

"This place is wonderful," Nicolette said. "You must be quite a powerful man."

"I have many powerful connections," he said proudly. "I have been in business here for decades. And I have seen my fair share of pretty girls, but you," he said, slowly, "are one of the prettiest."

Nicolette leaned towards him a bit. "I'm sure your wife is very lovely," she said softly.

"Yes, of course." Farouk nervously bit his lip.

"Does she treat you well?"

Before Farouk could respond, the door opened, and Rafael appeared with his mother. She was in her fifties but slim and well-kept. Not unattractive at all. But Nicolette knew what lurked inside Mr. Farouk's mind.

"I'd like you to meet my mother," Rafael said. "I owe her my life."

"A pleasure," she said with a slight bow. "My name is Abilah, but you may call me Abby."

Nicolette smiled. Abilah was very graceful, and her face, though showing some age, was vibrant and healthy.

Once they were seated, they ate heartily, and the majority of the time was spent by Nicolette and Rafael conversing about everything under the sun. His mother was beaming with pride in her son, while Rafael's father kept sneaking his eyes away to stare at Nicolette.

Finally, when all the dishes were cleared, Rafael stood and cleared his throat.

"I'm afraid it's getting late and we'll have to turn in for the night. But for you, Suzette, we have a private hotel suite at the resort across the way that you're welcome to use. If you need anything, just pick up the phone and ask."

"Thank you very much for the meal," Nicolette said emphatically. "Everything was delicious."

Rafael's mother stood also and smiled. "I will retire as well. It's been a long day. Suzette, it was such a pleasure to meet you."

"The pleasure's all mine, Abilah."

. . . .

The next evening, they arranged to have dinner again.

"You know, Rafael, I really like this girl."

Rafael smiled at his mother. "She's incredible. Every time I talk to her, I learn something new about her."

"Do you think she's the right one for you?" Abilah moved around the dinner table, laying out dishware as she talked.

"It's hard to say for sure," Rafael said, "but she's a better person than anyone else I've met."

"I know times change. I want you to know your father and I will be happy with whomever you choose."

"That won't be difficult," Rafael said with a smile. "I don't think you could find better."

The doorbell rang, and Rafael heard his father answer the door. Moments later, he appeared with Nicollette, who was wearing a rather short evening gown.

"Ah, good to see you!" Rafael's mother said. "I'll be right back."

Rafael leaned in and kissed Nicolette on the cheek, and pulled out a chair for her to sit. The men followed suit, and when Abilah returned, she sat to the right of her husband.

As servants brought out the first course, Rafael started discussing business with his father.

"I understand you're leaving town this week?"

"That's correct. I must travel to the coast to speak with my import manager."

"Could you not make a phone call?" Rafael asked.

"That is not the kind of talking-to he needs," Farouk replied. "These people don't know how to run anything. I have to attend to it myself, or it won't be done properly."

"But surely you can't do that for everything," Rafael shot back.

"I *think*," Farouk said, lowering his voice, "that I know what I'm doing. I suggest you pay more attention to your studies."

"So!" Nicollette said brightly. "When will you be returning?"

"That depends," Farouk said. "It might take a while."

"Rafael is leaving as well, right?"

"I am," Rafael said mid-chew. "I have to return to London before the next semester begins."

"That means," Nicolette said, locking eyes with Farouk, "that I'll have time to enjoy the resort. Alone."

"It won't be any trouble," Abilah said. "We've always got a few rooms open. You can stay as long as you like."

"I appreciate your hospitality," Nicolette replied. "You've been so kind to me. I wish there was some way I could repay you."

"That's not necessary," Abilah said. "Just let the staff know when you're ready to check out. The room is yours until then."

"Thank you, again." Nicolette carefully watched Farouk's responses to her hints. She wasn't sure he would catch on, but the opportunity was definitely there.

As they finished eating, Rafael stood. "An excellent meal as always, mother." He reached down, picked up her hand, and kissed it lightly. "Your cooking never ceases to amaze me."

"You're such a sweet boy," Abilah said. "But your flattery won't get you more dessert."

Rafael and Abilah laughed heartily. Nicolette loved the fact that he and his mother had such a good relationship, which made it all the more frustrating that his father was so corrupt. But that wouldn't be a problem much longer.

"Thank you again," Rafael said, motioning for Nicollette to join him. "We must be going for the night, as I have to leave first thing in the morning. But I wanted to spend a few minutes with Suzette before it got too late."

"Good night," Abilah said. "I hope you enjoyed dinner."

Farouk only stared as Nicolette leaned over to pick up her purse, giving him a full show of her cleavage.

As Rafael turned to escort Nicolette out, she looked at Mr. Farouk and offered a subtle grin. She didn't bother to wait for a response.

• • • •

At the hotel, Nicolette was just finishing drying her hair when she was startled by a knock at the door.

She quickly walked to the door, only wearing a nightgown, and opened it.

"Kamal!"

"Anyone else in here?" Kamal asked quietly.

"No," Nicolette said. "Not yet."

"Good." He stepped inside, closed the door, and sighed. "I'm glad Rafael's not here."

Nicolette raised an eyebrow. "What if he was?"

"I don't want to talk about that," Kamal said. "That's not why I'm here."

"Did you bring what you needed?"

"I did," Kamal said, swinging a backpack around. "This is what you're interested in." He reached in the bag and pulled out a small glass bottle with a white label on it.

"How much do I need?"

"Just four or five drops will knock him out for a few minutes. Just long enough."

"OK, got it." She walked over to where the kitchenette was, and put a glass Champagne flute on the counter. She then opened a Champagne bottle, and filled the glass with bubbly.

"To justice," Nicolette said.

"To justice." Kamal repeated with a nod.

• • • •

About an hour later, around ten o'clock, another knock came.

This time, Nicolette looked through the peephole.

"Come in," she called, stepping away from the door.

The door opened, and Mr. Farouk stood there, with lust in his eyes. Nicolette knew that look all too well.

Turning so that her nightgown didn't quite cover everything, Nicolette smiled. "Oh, I wasn't expecting you, Mr. Farouk."

"Don't play dumb with me," he replied. "My son, Rafael, might be naive, but I know a fine woman when I see one."

Nicolette sauntered over to the table, making sure to take her time. "Could I interest you in a drink?"

"That would be lovely," he said, his breathing getting more labored.

She returned with a Champagne glass, and handed it to him.

"Thank you," he wheezed, still breathing heavily. As she turned to go back to the kitchen, he reached out and firmly grabbed her ass, causing her to squeal and jump a little.

"Drink up," she said smoothly. "You're in for a night you won't forget."

• • • •

"Where am I?"

The room slowly came into focus. Farouk was sitting in a chair, his hands tied behind his back, his legs strapped to the chair's legs. His mouth was filled with the horrible metallic taste of bile, and his shirt was covered in vomit.

"You're still here," Nicolette said. "Can you see me now?"

Farouk squinted, trying to clear his eyes. "Is that you? Suzette?"

"No. There is no Suzette."

"Wh—what?"

Nicolette appeared, now dressed in jeans and a t-shirt. Her hair was pulled up in a ponytail. Her smile was gone.

"Do you recognize me?"

Farouk shook his head.

With as much strength as she could muster, Nicolette reared back and slapped him across the face, leaving a cherry red handprint across it. His eyes blurred again.

"TAKE ANOTHER LOOK!"

She leaned in and stared into his eyes. "Remember?! The orphanage?!"

At first, there was nothing. Then his eyes twitched. Then they went wide.

"No, no . . . that's . . . impossible!"

Nicolette stood up straight and glared. "You're so very, very wrong."

Then there were rough hands forcing a ball gag into his mouth. He struggled to no avail. Once it was done, he just sat there. Trembling. Drool ran down his chin.

Kamal appeared, wearing gloves and holding a crowbar.

"Is there anything else you want to tell him before I take his life?"

Nicolette closed her eyes, took a deep breath, and sighed.

"Everything you did to me, I will repay you for."

"*Mmmmmph!*"

Without warning, a flying fist connected with Farouk's nose, shattering it, and spraying blood everywhere. His eyes rolled back in his head.

Kamal gripped a crowbar with both hands. He waited for the coursing pain to bring Farouk back. Once Kamal saw his eyes, he rained down blows, one after the next. Smashing shins, feet, and arms, each one connecting with a sickening *thud*.

The muffled screaming continued as the beating went on until Farouk ran out of breath, gasped for air through the blood and vomit, and started again.

Ten minutes later, most of the bones in Farouk's legs were broken. His skin swelled purple.

But Kamal wasn't done. Nicolette had backed away, at first to avoid being splattered with blood. Now she wondered if Kamal was actually going to let the man die.

And then, there was a pause. Kamal stopped, mid-swing, and backed away. Farouk's head writhed back and forth, barely breathing through the gag as he faded in and out of consciousness.

"You can't escape punishment by passing out," Kamal hissed. "I won't allow it."

"*Mmmmph . . .*"

Kamal reached over, unsnapped the strap holding the gag on, and yanked it out of his mouth. For a few moments, all Farouk could do was try to catch his breath.

Nicolette stepped closer. "Kamal," she whispered, "aren't you going to get it over with?"

Kamal turned slowly. His eyes narrowed.

"Yes." Turning back to Farouk, Kamal cracked a wide smile. "But not before we exact our pound of flesh, isn't that right?"

"P—please. Please . . . I never . . . never killed any—"

"Oh, but you did," Kamal sneered. "You destroyed more lives than anyone I know. You stole the lives of little girls who were powerless to stop you."

"I'm sorry. I just—I need a doctor."

"It's too late for apologies," Kamal said. "Now is the time to pay the debt you owe."

Kamal picked up the gag and re-secured it in Farouk's mouth. Farouk's eyes widened in desperation. He knew what was coming.

With that, Kamal pulled out a large combat knife and plunged it into Farouk's crotch. The gag could not contain the scream. Farouk tried to close his legs, but shattered bones could do nothing.

Kamal then took the knife and roughly cut away most of Farouk's pants, revealing his now partially-severed genitals. More blood ran down his legs and onto the floor.

Kamal paused, holding the knife at the ready, until Farouk managed to focus his eyes enough to see him.

"It's not a pound of flesh. But it's enough."

With a flick of his wrist, Kamal slammed the knife through Mr. Farouk and into the chair's seat with a thud.

Kamal reached down, picked up the bloody mass of severed genitals, and turned to Nicolette. Then Kamal held up his prize.

Nicolette grabbed her stomach. She retched violently and vomited all over Farouk's blood on the floor.

Everything dimmed. She stumbled backwards against the wall. Her legs gave way, and she collapsed into a heap. She watched as Kamal just stood there, slowly letting Farouk bleed out.

• • • •

The next thing Nicolette remembered was waking up and wondering if everything that had happened the night before was the worst nightmare she'd ever had.

She sat up in bed, still in her jeans and t-shirt, and looked around. There was no sign of blood anywhere.

"Good morning!"

The door opened and Kamal entered with a breakfast tray.

"I brought you something to eat. You looked really tired."

Nicolette just stared.

"What?" Kamal said, shrugging. "I knew you were hungry."

Nicolette shook her head, trying to wake herself up.

"Kamal, last night . . ."

"That's over and done with," Kamal said. "Now that he's out of the picture. Rafael will inherit everything. You'll be set for life."

Nicolette looked down at the breakfast tray, then back up at Kamal.

"OK. I'll get dressed and meet you downstairs."

"Great." Kamal turned and left, leaving Nicolette alone to try not to remember.

And it was then Nicolette realized that Kamal had turned into a monster.

And what was worse—he had trained her to become a monster as well. Except that she didn't enjoy seeing Farouk suffer. She wasn't even sure killing him was justice. It was clear, now, that Kamal was channeling all of his life's anger into the old man's broken, shattered body. Even thinking about it, remembering the look on his face, still turned her stomach.

Nicolette's feelings built until she shook. Then cried. And once the tears began, the pain flowed out and flowed out.

Kamal . . . she could no longer trust him. Maybe she never really could to begin with. Maybe Nicolette's own instincts had lied to her, too. For all these years.

CHAPTER 12

PART II
NOBODY

The night air was crisp and clear, leaving the starry sky unveiled. Kamal sat alone on his poolside patio, looking up into the sky. Occasionally, there was the distant *pop* of gunfire, followed by a faint siren. Kamal lifted a wine glass to his lips, inhaled for a second, and then took a sip.

Finally, when the glass was empty, Kamal sighed and stood up. All around him was a stone wall, fencing in a sprawling well-kept garden. A slight rustle of leaves in the wind caused him to snap back to reality.

He had come to Beirut because it was home. But here, surrounded by stone walls and iron fences, Kamal felt more alone than ever.

• • • •

"I can't believe this could have happened!" Rafael said, his voice quivering. "Who could have done such a thing? What monster?!"

Nicolette's face barely twitched. "I don't know. It's . . . it's . . . horrible."

"One of his business deals went bad. That's it. That's the only explanation." Rafael shook his head. "Got in with some bad people . . I . . . I just can't believe it."

Nicolette played the scene over again in her mind. She felt something she hadn't felt since childhood—sympathy.

Nicolette wrapped her arm around Rafael's shoulder and nodded to the detective. "Thank you for telling him."

The policeman tipped his hat and turned, walking away down the corridor.

"Let's go someplace," Nicolette said. "C'mon. There's nothing for you here."

Rafael sniffed, wiped his nose, and stood up. "You're right. I need to clear my head."

"Do you want to go home?"

"No," he said. "I know a better place."

They walked, arm in arm, out of the police station to the street, where Rafael's car was parked. They had come as fast as they could when they had gotten the news.

As they got in the car, Rafael paused and looked into Nicolette's eyes. "Are you okay?"

"I don't know. I'm honestly still processing it."

"I want to show you something that I think will give you an idea of some of the good things my father did." Rafael started the car's engine, and pulled away from the curb. "I know he wasn't a perfect father," he added, "but he wasn't all bad, either."

Nicolette remained silent as the city lights slid past. She wasn't even sure what she believed any more.

In the darkness behind them, unnoticed, a car quietly followed them through the streets.

• • • •

Rafael eventually stopped in front of a large wrought iron gate, framed by rustic stone walls. He pressed a button on his visor, and the gate beeped, and slowly parted.

Nicolette couldn't quite make out what was beyond, until they entered and rounded a copse of trees. There, sprawling down the hill and surrounding fields, was an honest-to-God castle. The grounds and gardens were lit up with soft lighting, highlighting where everything was without casting harsh shadows. The outer courtyard wall curved and swirled around the castle like a living, breathing thing. A retaining wall curved out into the edge of the waterfront, marking a stark boundary between land and sea. The blocky walls and towers topped with parapets looked like they were straight out of a fairy tale.

"Incredible." Nicolette gasped. "Is this yours?"

Rafael smiled. "It belongs to the family, if that's what you're asking." He pointed to the tallest tower. "That's where I used to sit as a child and just watch boats pass up and down the coast."

He pulled the car into the courtyard, shut off the engine, and turned to Nicolette.

"This place is very special to me, and I wanted to share it with you. Someone also special to me."

Nicolette smiled but quickly dropped her gaze.

"I have something to tell you."

"Yes, my love?"

Nicolette let out a long sigh. "I have spent my entire life pushing down my feelings. For years, I just used people. They meant nothing to me."

Rafael leaned in closer and motioned for her to continue.

"But when I met you, it was different. *You* were different. And I couldn't—I mean, I found myself . . . And then your father . . . He . . ."

"Yes?"

"I don't know how else to say it," Nicolette finally said. "I want you. To be with you. You, Rafael. I've never met . . . anyone like you before. It makes me want to stay with you—" she looked up and smiled. "I want to stay with you forever. And I want to make your pain go away. All of it. Forever."

Rafael tenderly reached out, put his hand on her cheek, and drew her in close.

"I would go to the ends of the earth for you," he whispered. "Will you stay with me?"

She could only nod. Then their lips met, sending jolts of excitement through her body she had never felt.

The kiss ended slowly, leaving Nicolette shaken. Nothing else mattered to her. This was real, here and now.

"Come with me," Rafael said. He opened the door, walked around the car, and as Nicolette stepped out, he swung her up into his arms, holding her close.

"This seems familiar," she laughed. She tucked her head to his chest, and held on tightly.

Rafael made his way to the castle's main door, and gently set her on her feet. He opened the door, grabbed her hand, and stepped inside.

As they disappeared into the keep, a shadow appeared in the soft glow around the entrance. After a long pause, it moved into the doorway, entered, and closed the door behind it with a clack.

• • • •

The interior of the castle was decorated with historical furnishings, nineteenth century appointments, and antique lighting. Kamal looked around and held his breath, but he heard nothing.

He walked slowly up the sweeping circular staircase, making sure not to alert anyone of his presence. The place was large, but fairly simple in design. At the top of the staircase, Kamal saw one of the landings was larger than the other, and headed that way.

The walkway wrapped around the foyer and into a long hallway, lined with finely decorated wooden doors. Carefully, he stepped down the hall, listening intently.

Towards the end of the hall, at the last door, Kamal could make out what sounded like voices—a man and a woman. But it wasn't a conversation.

He cautiously put his ear to the door and listened. Bits and pieces of sound came through, and he began to put together pieces.

"Suzette . . ." Rafael let out a low moan.

"I've loved you since the moment I met you,"

There was some rustling, and more hushed whispers. The time seemed to stretch on forever.

Kamal's heart pounded in his chest. He knew what was happening, and in a way, he was happy for Nicolette. But there was something about it that wasn't right. She was enjoying it.

The sounds behind the door increased in intensity, until there was a muffled cry as they consummated their passion. Kamal could feel the blood rushing to his face as Nicolette's cries became more and more intense, rising in volume and pitch.

Kamal clenched his fists. Nicolette, the girl he had saved, making love to the only man she had given her heart to. Didn't she belong to him? Kamal had protected her with his life, and this was how she repaid him.

The frantic noises twisted something deep down inside Kamal. His heart was being torn to pieces by the only person he had ever cared about. Deep pain like he had never known before flooded his soul.

As the sounds increased in intensity, so did Kamal's anguish. The only thing that truly mattered in his life was now gone, stolen by another man. Kamal thought about how horrible and cruel fate was in coming back around, and in a moment, he finally snapped.

Kamal took a step back, sucked in a deep breath, and with a shout of rage, kicked the door open.

There, naked and sprawled out on the bed, were Rafael and Nicolette, intertwined mid-thrust.

Nicolette screamed, as Rafael jumped up and whirled around. Nicolette grabbed a sheet and pulled it around herself.

Kamal stood there, breathing heavily, his face twisted into a scowl and his shoulders hunched over like a gargoyle. To Nicolette, he was almost unrecognizable.

Rafael looked at Nicolette, then back to Kamal. "Who the hell are you?"

"Kamal!" Nicolette shrieked. "What are you doing here?!"

"Suzette, you know this guy?" Rafael frowned. "Look, I don't know how you got in here, but you need to leave—*right. now*. Or I'll call the police."

Kamal's eyes narrowed, and his scowl slowly transformed into a gruesome smile. Nicolette could see his eyes were empty, like there was nothing behind them—just pure, unadulterated rage, pain and hatred.

"Kamal, leave us alone!" Nicolette's voice wavered. "I'm happy! Isn't that what you wanted?"

"Oh, is that right, *Nicolette?*" Kamal hissed. "You finally had enough of me?"

Rafael lifted an eyebrow.

"That's right," Kamal said. "Her real name . . . Nicolette." He pointed a finger at her. "You weren't going to tell him the truth, were you, *Nicolette?*"

Nicolette's face changed, and her lips turned white. "It doesn't matter what he calls me!" She looked up at Rafael. "Besides, the girl you knew as Nicolette is dead. I'm not your plaything any more."

"Is that true?" Rafael said.

"Yes, it's true," Nicolette said. "But I want to leave all that behind me. My old life, the lies, the running . . ."

Rafael slowly held his hands up, and stepped between them. "Look, I don't care what your problem with her is, but you can rest assured she'll be taken care of." He stared intently at Kamal, and added, "I think you need to leave now."

There was a second of tension, as Kamal ran the words through his head. When he spoke, there was pain and anger like Nicolette had never heard before.

"I saved her!" Kamal, his brow furrowed, jabbed a finger at Rafael. "I pulled her out of the slums! I made a life for us together! I gave her everything she ever wanted!"

"No." Rafael bristled. "No, you didn't."

"*I saved her life!*" Kamal shouted. "What could you possibly give her that I can't?"

Rafael leaned in closer to Kamal and shook his head.

"You can't ever give her real love." He straightened himself and looked back at Nicolette, smiling.

"I love her more than anything!" Kamal said hotly. "I sacrificed everything I had for her!" He balled up his fists and snarled. "*She belongs to me!*"

Rafael chuckled and shook his head.

"Not any more. She's made her choice."

"Kamal," Nicolette said, "please, just go. There's nothing more to say."

"So this is how it's going to be?" Kamal said, his voice cracking slightly.

Before Nicolette could say a word, Kamal reached behind his back and produced a revolver, pointing it straight at Rafael.

"I'll make your choice easier!"

"NOOO!" Nicolette jumped up and attempted to throw herself at Kamal. She was too slow.

The shot reverberated in the stone-walled room.

Rafael's look of shock went slack, as he slumped to the floor. Blood began rapidly spreading from the wound.

"You goddamn bastard!" Nicolette made it to her feet and threw herself at Kamal, flailing her fists at him. "How could you! You monster!"

Kamal fended off her blows with his free hand. "You could have never been happy with him," he said. "You're too corrupted! Too dirty. He'd never be satisfied with you!"

"Is that right, you coward?" Nicolette fumed. "What would you know about love and satisfaction? You've never been able to get your mind out of the slums! All you think about, all you care about, is screwing over and cheating everyone!" She pulled back and punched him a few more times. "I'm sick of your games, Kamal." She looked down at Rafael's lifeless body, and began to sob uncontrollably.

"I did you a favor," Kamal snarled. "You owe me."

"You didn't save me, you bastard son of a whore! You destroyed my life!" she screamed, her voice breaking "I hate you! I hate everything you've made me do, and I hate what you tried to turn me into!"

For a fraction of a moment, Kamal's rage disappeared.

"I was only trying to save you," he said softly. "I did it because I love you."

"You don't love me!" Nicolette shouted. "You never did! You just used me, like you used everyone else!" Her nostrils flared as she turned and full-armed slapped him. "I don't love you, Kamal! I never loved you! And I never asked you to do any of this for me!"

Kamal flinched, but said nothing.

"I hate you, Kamal! I never want to see you again as long as I live!" She turned and walked to the bed where her dress was hastily dropped. "You're worse than a filthy dog in the gutter, laying in its own vomit. Everything you touch turns to shit!"

Kamal's rage instantly reappeared.

Nicolette just barely managed to turn around as Kamal raised the pistol and fired.

The shot hit her in the neck, blowing flesh and blood all over the wall. She collapsed to her knees, blood gushing everywhere. Her hands went to her neck to stop the bleeding. There was too much. As she slid to the floor, her face going pale, she tried to speak, but could only gurgle. Finally, she managed to mouth something to Kamal.

"Go to hell."

Within seconds, the blood loss caused Nicolette to pass out, her labored breathing slowing until the room was silent.

Kamal looked down at his hand, still holding the pistol. All of a sudden, the veil of rage lifted, and he saw what had happened.

Rafael and Nicolette's naked, lifeless bodies lay in a massive pool of blood. Crimson splashes covered the bed. Kamal's shoes, standing in the blood, had turned red.

Kamal's brain reeled. It was like waking up from a horrible nightmare, except everything was real. The ringing in his ears was real. The warm liquid soaking into his shoes was real. Nicolette's hair, once beautiful and feminine, was matted and soaked through with blood like an animal shot in the wild.

Kamal's hands began to tremble. When he realized it, he tried to hold them still, but they wouldn't stop shaking. His entire body violently spasmed, as his emotions broke through the walls that had been up for so long.

"Oh my God . . . what have I done?" he sobbed, dropping to his knees with a wet thud. "Nicolette . . .what have I done?!"

Kamal saw his hand raise, involuntarily lifting the pistol until it was pointed up at his own chin. He felt the hot barrel pressing into his flesh. His hand, still trembling, squeezed the gun tightly so as to not drop it.

"I failed you, Nicol," he said in between gasps. "My sweet, sweet, nicol . . ."

It would only take a single twitch of a muscle to end it all. Everything he had done, all the wrongs he had caused, all the horrible things he had

CHAPTER 12 - PART II NOBODY

done—gone in an instant. The pain would finally cease. All he had to do was pull one finger on the trigger.

An eternity passed as Kamal's heart pounded. Nothing seemed better than being able to escape all this mess, to finally end it all.

But something kept him from doing it. Kamal concentrated, and tried to pull the trigger just once more, but the muscles in his hand refused to cooperate. He even tried thinking the word *squeeze*, but nothing happened.

"Goddammit!" He shouted and threw the gun to the floor, where it clattered and came to rest.

And then something in the back of his mind—something he had been carrying since his days at the orphanage—kicked in. He ran.

Kamal, still struggling to control his grief, stumbled out into the castle's hallway, leaving bloody footprints as he went. He staggered down the stairs and out the foyer, into the cold, dark night.

Illuminated by moonlight, Kamal could see the driveway disappearing through the woods. The only thing he could think of was disappearing into the night.

His eyes full of tears, he broke into a sprint, taking off into the trees. He had to get away, to run, to erase the horrible memory from his mind.

No matter how fast he ran, Kamal knew the nightmare would follow him forever.

To Be Continued . . .

To follow Kamal's story, follow the author on Instagram. There you can be the first to see breaking news about the upcoming sequel to *The Wolf of the Middle East*.

www.instagram.com/hakeemalzayn

www.ingramcontent.com/pod-product-compliance
Lightning Source LLC
Chambersburg PA
CBHW020155090426
42734CB00008B/825